Systematic Word Study

for Grades 2-3

**An Easy Weekly Routine for Teaching Hundreds of New Words
to Develop Strong Readers, Writers, & Spellers**

Cheryl M. Sigmon

■ SCHOLASTIC

New York • Toronto • London • Auckland • Sydney
Mexico City • New Delhi • Hong Kong • Buenos Aires

Dedication

This book is dedicated to second- and third-grade teachers,
who give the gift of word knowledge to students each and every day.

And to my granddaughter, Meg Truluck,
who is currently a fifth grader learning firsthand about the power of words
from her parents and teachers. May you put words to good use in your life!

Finally, to my husband,
who supports my efforts and enriches my life in so many ways.

*

Cover design by Jaime Lucero
Cover photograph by Getty Images/Fuse
Interior design by Sarah Morrow
Editor: Sarah Glasscock
Copy Editor: Jeannie Hutchins

ISBN: 978-0-545-24160-1
Copyright © 2011 Cheryl M. Sigmon
All rights reserved.
Printed in the U.S.A.

1 2 3 4 5 6 7 8 9 10   40   17 16 15 14 13 12 11

Contents

Introduction

Indeed, one of the most persistent findings in reading research is the extent to which students' vocabulary knowledge relates strongly to their reading comprehension and overall academic success.

—Fran Lehr, Jean Osborn, & Elfrieda H. Hiebert

With most basic print and language concepts under their belts, second- and third-grade students are ready to move into more sophisticated aspects of word study. The lessons in this book are designed to help you engage students with words not only by looking at the semantic features of the words but also by gaining greater understanding of the nuances and relationships these words present. At second and third grade, students have the capacity to appreciate the complex nature of words—their multiple meanings, their use in idioms, their meaningful word parts and derivations, and the multifaceted relationships among words. Powerful instruction in some necessary high-frequency words, content vocabulary, and general academic vocabulary are embedded in each weekly lesson. The lessons provide a systematic, daily instruction in words, even within a limited time frame, which will motivate and engage your learners. Each lesson is structured to make the best use of the precious little time you have in your classroom to teach all that you must teach. Most important, the lessons will positively impact your students' confidence in communicating effectively and ultimately will increase their level of literacy achievement.

Which Words Need to Be Taught and Why

The Power of High-Frequency Words

Certain words in the English language are, of necessity, repeated frequently. In fact, three little words—*I, and, the*—account for 10 percent of all printed words! The top 25 words account for one-third of all print. And, amazingly, 107 of the top high-frequency words account for half of all printed text (Zeno, Ivens, Millard, & Duvvuri, 1995)! These 107 high-frequency words are included in the first book of this series, which is geared to grade 1. Students usually master these words in first grade; however, if they don't, you will need to provide additional opportunities for students to master those words, which will aid their reading and writing fluency. Otherwise, the gap is likely to grow as students move from grade to grade. As the list of high-frequency words changes from grade to grade, it increasingly includes a number of words with irregular spellings that pose potential problems for struggling students.

How do we make good use of our knowledge about high-frequency words? It stands to reason that the more words readers and writers know automatically, the more fluently they will read and write. Building automaticity, or quickness, with high-frequency words means that the reader/writer does not have to stop and consciously labor over decoding or encoding to accomplish these processes. Our goal, even with the simple high-frequency words, is not merely to have students memorize the words for a test on Friday, but rather to have them process these words to the extent that they know the words automatically for the long term. This automaticity comes only through repetition and multisensory engagement with the words and their features. And you will see that the activities in these lessons do just that—engage each and every learner!

Beyond building desirable fluency in reading and writing, the greater benefit might be that the cognitive focus of the reader or writer can then be directed toward more difficult aspects of the processes involved—reading comprehension or writing craft. With basic sight words under control, students' minds are free to figure out relationships in text, characters' motives, the best way to begin or end a piece of writing, or the voice they need to use to convey a certain message. Depth of understanding in reading and writing stems first from the small but mighty word!

In this book, high-frequency words still receive emphasis, although the words used in these lessons are less common than the high-frequency words taught in kindergarten and first grade. The lessons start with a balance—half high-frequency words and half content and/or academic words. As lessons progress, they are weighted on the side of content and academic vocabulary. From the first lesson, students need to use critical-thinking skills for answering the questions you pose about the words. A few of the words in the activities may even be a bit difficult for some of your students, but those segments of the lessons are brief. The activities will challenge more advanced students without diminishing the interest and motivation of students who are less prepared for the challenge.

So, the high-frequency word itself is not a critical part of these lessons. What is critical is having students process the word so that it becomes automatic and using the word as a starting point to delve into more complex word issues.

Including Content Vocabulary and General Academic Vocabulary

In addition to high-frequency words, the 35 lessons in this book include a number of critical vocabulary words from content areas—math, science, social studies, language arts—and from specialized curriculum areas such as music and art. The lists provided are, of course, not inclusive of all content area words to which you should expose your students; however, they represent major concepts commonly taught in second- and third-grade curricula.

The lessons also include general academic words—words that will benefit students because they are shared among all disciplines—such as *directions, general, specific, question, summarize*, and *solve*. By exposing students often to these words, they will develop a familiarity with them. This is crucial, since students will need to understand these words to function well in the school day and beyond.

The juxtaposition of familiar high-frequency words and less familiar content and academic words will help make the latter less intimidating to students as they attempt to understand and practice the set of words in each lesson. All words are analyzed and explored in a number of different ways to be both interesting and thought-provoking.

The content areas represented most often in this book are math, science, social studies, and language arts. Additionally, a few character education words and art and health vocabulary are included. The correct spelling of these words, many of which are big words that might be difficult for some of your students, is not as important at this level as the correct spelling of the high-frequency words. For example, having all students spell *decomposer* without fail is far less important than having them know the meaning of this science word and relying upon their knowledge of its word parts, which can transfer into other words that have *de-*, *com-*, and *-er* chunks. Researchers have shown that a mere 14 prefixes and suffixes account for approximately 75 percent of all affixed words (White, Sowell, & Yanagihara, 1989)! Just think of the power of teaching students these tiny bits of information. You give them the keys to unlock the meaning of the majority of the more difficult words that they will encounter in their studies.

Many of the academic words and some of the high-frequency words are additionally challenging to students because they have multiple meanings. In fact, approximately 70 percent of the most commonly used words that we draw upon in our everyday lives possess more than one meaning (Bromley, 2007). The most common meanings of words in these lessons is discussed explicitly.

General academic words are those that are shared among all educators in your school—*where, solution, predict, fact/opinion, reliable, summarize*, among others. Second- and third-grade students need to know these words, understand their nuances, and be able to read and write them.

Concepts Taught and Reinforced in These Lessons

Each lesson revolves around a five-day plan. Within this time period, students engage in a number of hands-on activities that will increase their word knowledge. Further, the lessons provide hands-on, explicit instruction in most, if not all, of the state standards I reviewed before compiling this book and creating the activities. The following elements appear in each lesson.

Day 1: Meet the Words

Introduce each of the 8 words for the week as students observe and manipulate their corresponding word cards. In this activity, students will do the following:

- recognize each of the 8 words for the week

- learn why the words are important to know—whether they are high-frequency or content words

- realize how their knowledge of the words can transfer to their reading and writing

- learn how the spelling patterns of some words help us read and write many other words

- manipulate letters and sounds to create new words

- learn how to use the features of the words to their advantage, such as how grasping the meanings of word parts can help unlock the meanings of other words

- understand the language of word study—syllables, consonants, vowels, plural/singular, tenses, prefixes, and suffixes

- learn the derivations of some words, which is both interesting and useful in word study

Day 2: Word Whittle

You share clues about the characteristics shared by several of the words. As you give each clue, students "whittle" down or narrow the pool of words until only one word remains. In this lesson, students will do the following:

- observe the physical characteristics of words—such as tall letters, letters that extend below the line, and the word length

- count syllables

- listen for sounds made by certain letters and combinations of letters

- recognize useful spelling patterns

- analyze relationships among words

Stump the Class (a secondary activity)

In this activity, you issue a challenge for each student, pair, or small group to analyze the 8 words for the week to determine relationships among them. Students use critical-thinking skills to find and categorize these relationships. There are no parameters on the relationships they can explore—physical features, semantic features, content-related connections, or more personal connections they might make. Students may even relate the words to popular culture—which can help them process the words on a deeper level! The real challenge here is for students to find unique categories that will stump their classmates when they share their word groupings. This activity requires students to operate at the top level of Bloom's Taxonomy, where they do the following:

- create, evaluate, and analyze words and their connections

- categorize words based on connections

- articulate the connections to others

Day 3: Word Builder

In this activity, each student manipulates letter strips at your direction. They build many words, working up to a single word that can be spelled with all the letters. In building words, students will learn to do the following:

- manipulate letters and sounds to create words

- use patterns of language to help spell new words

- apply certain rules for spelling

- practice the language of word study—prefixes, suffixes, affixes, consonants, vowels, and so on

- attempt to build multisyllabic words with your guidance

Day 4: Rhymer

The Day 3: Word Builder activity is a springboard into this activity. Students work with the spelling patterns they discovered in Word Builder. They take more responsibility for their learning and rely less on your assistance. Here, students do the following:

- manipulate letters and sounds to create new words

- use patterns of language to spell new words

- apply spelling rules they have learned

- work with words on a more independent level

Day 5: Word Smart

The Word Smart challenge is the culmination of everything that students have learned about these words throughout the week. They demonstrate an understanding of the following:

- physical and semantic features

- word parts/affixes

- hidden words

- relationships and connections

- parts of speech

- word meaning

Basically, students show that they understand the words, have processed the words in a new and different way, and can have fun with and be challenged by words as well. Lessons become more difficult, but they always remain multilevel, in order to meet the needs of all your students.

On each day, you will teach word knowledge that empowers students to widen their grasp and use of the words—far beyond the immediate lesson.

Word Chart

Week	Words	Content Words	Features
1	been, off, cold, tell, publish, unknown, unlikely, interpret (publishers)	high-frequency words; language arts words; academic words	spelling patterns -*ush*, -*ub*, -*ur*, -*ip*; consonant blends (*shr*-, *bl*-, -*sh*, *sl*-); suffixes -*er*, -*s*; prefix *un*-; plurals
2	work, first, goes, does, adjective, county, rural, urban (suburban)	high-frequency words; language arts word; social studies words	spelling patterns -*ub*, -*urn*; prefix *sub*-; rime and rhyme of *does*/*goes*
3	them, your, their, pronoun, us, compare, contrast, dissolve (similarities)	high-frequency words; language arts words; science words	spelling patterns -*ail*, -*ale*, -*ir*; homophones; suffix -*er*; pronouns and nouns
4	its, around, don't, right, plural, fraction, one-fourth, one-third (fractions)	high-frequency words; math words; language arts words	spelling patterns -*an*, -*at*, -*act*, -*orn*, -*ost*, -*aft*; plurals; hyphens; consonant blends *sc*-, *fr*-, -*st*, *pl*-; differentiating *its* and *it's*
5	would, green, call, sleep, revise, conflict, landmark, symbol (skyscraper)	high-frequency words; language arts words; math words	spelling patterns -*ack*, -*ap*, -*ar*, -*ark*, -*are*; long vowel/consonant /silent *e*; compound words
6	five, wash, know, before, edit, resource, energy, nonrenewable (resourceful)	high-frequency words; science words; language arts words	spelling patterns -*ore*, -*ure*, -*our*; prefixes *non*-, *re*-; suffixes -*able*, -*ful*; same rime pattern but different rhyme (*four*, *our*); *kn* with silent *k*
7	where, were, when, or, prefixes, prewrite, distance, inches (measurement)	high-frequency words, language arts words, math words,	spelling patterns -*et*, -*eam*, -*ame*, -*ust*, -*ate*, -*ear*; suffixes -*ern*, -*en*, -*er*; plurals; meaning relationships; homophones
8	then, could, ask, every, draft, singular, yard, foot (carpenters)	high-frequency words, math words	spelling patterns -*est*, -*an*, -*ar*, -*ace*, -*ent*; homophones; multiple meanings; suffixes -*er* and -*s*; consonant blends; regular and irregular plurals
9	write, always, made, gave, plot, infer, investigate, scientist (investigator)	high-frequency words; language arts words; academic words; science words	spelling patterns -*ave*, -*ove*, -*eat*; prefix *in*-; suffixes -*ing*, -*or*, -*er*, -*ist*

10	very, buy, those, use, suffixes, dimensions, perimeter, circle (dimensions)	high-frequency words; language arts words; math words	spelling patterns -ose, -ine, -end, -ide; some rime patterns have different rhyme patterns; plurals; verb tense
11	fast, pull, both, duty, volunteer, contribution, privilege, government (democracy)	high-frequency words; social studies words; character-ed words	spelling patterns -am, -are, -ay; suffixes -tion, -ment
12	sit, which, read, glossary, evaporation, barometer, atmosphere, cycle (atmosphere)	high-frequency words; academic words; science words	spelling patterns -ap, -ot, -eat, -ear, -eam; prefixes re-, pre-; word relationships
13	why, found, because, economy, distribution, export, import, abbreviation (abbreviations)	high-frequency words; language arts words; social studies words	spelling patterns -ain, -ave, -it; prepositions; prefix re-; suffixes -or, -tion
14	best, upon, these, predict, symmetry, congruent, polygon, intersecting (triangle)	high-frequency words; math words	spelling patterns -ain, -int, -are, -ear, -ing; consonant blend st-; verb tenses; superlatives
15	sing, wish, many, habitat, offspring, parent, depend, heredity (generation)	high-frequency words; science words	spelling patterns -ot, -ain, -one, -eat, -een, -ore, -age; colors; verb tenses; rhyme/rime difference
16	if, long, about, product, produce, services, goods, barter, (purchasing)	high-frequency words; social studies words	spelling patterns -ash, -ush; adding -ing to words; multiple meanings
17	got, six, never, sequential, fiction, nonfiction, fable, purpose (mysteries)	high-frequency words; language arts words; academic words	spelling pattern -im; word endings
18	seven, eight, tonight, compost, organism, consumer, producer, decomposer (decomposer)	high-frequency words; science words; math words	spelling patterns -oop, -oom, -ome, -op, -ode, -ope; endings -er, -ed
19	myself, much, keep, fact, opinion, angle, parallel, perpendicular (mathematics)	high-frequency words; math words; language arts words	spelling patterns -at, -ase, -eat, -ash, -eam; angle/angel confusion; prefix mis-; /ch/ sound

Systematic Word Study for Grades 2–3 © 2011 by Cheryl M. Sigmon, Scholastic Teaching Resources

20	try, start, highest, global, climate, agriculture, scarcity, manufacturing (manufacture)	high-frequency words; social studies words; science words	spelling patterns -*ace*, -*arm*, -*art*, -*ate*, -*ear*, -*ame*; prefixes *re*-, *un*-; superlatives
21	bring, drink, only, declarative, exclamatory, orbit, solar, rotation (astronomy)	high-frequency words; language arts words; science words	spelling patterns -*any*, -*ay*, -*art*, -*osy*; word part -*ast*; -*y* ending
22	better, hold, warm, interrogative, imperative, quart, pound, ounce (hamburgers)	high-frequency words; language arts words; math words	spelling patterns -*ug*, -*um*, -*ag*, -*ush*, -*ash*, -*arm*, -*ars*
23	full, done, light, culture, ancestor, ethnic, population, artifact (population)	high-frequency words; science words; social studies words	spelling patterns -*op*, -*ail*, -*ain*, -*ool*, -*out*; homophones; suffix -*tion*
24	pick, cut, hurt, poetry, stanza, endangered, predator, prey (alligators)	high-frequency words; language arts words; science words	spelling patterns -*all*, -*oll*, -*oast*, -*it*, -*air*; rime/rhyme differences; word part *pred*; suffix -*or*
25	kind, enough, Internet, reliable, citation, keyboard, mouse, source (keyboards)	high-frequency words; academic words; technology words	spelling patterns -*ad*, -*ake*, -*ark*, -*ask*, -*y*; past-tense verbs
26	carry, small, table, possessive, area, perimeter, capacity, elapsed (guinea pigs)	high-frequency words; academic words; math words; language arts words	spelling patterns -*age*, -*ip*, -*ap*, -*ain*, -*ag*, -*ang*; word endings -*ing*, -*s*
27	show, whether, weather, threaten, thrive, thermometer, discuss, beautiful (hurricanes)	high-frequency words; science words; academic words	spelling patterns -*ash*, -*ush*, -*ace*, -*air*, -*each*, -*ear*, -*ane*; word endings -*er*, -*es*; word part *therm*; *whether/weather* confusion
28	far, strange, cause, effect, hemisphere, geography, landforms, arid (geologists)	high-frequency words; language arts words; social studies words	spelling patterns -*oss*, -*oil*, -*ool*, -*ist*, -*ot*; word parts *geo*, *ologist*, *graph*, *hemi*, *sphere*; verb tenses
29	draw, clean, round, conclusion, details, decimal, equivalent, estimate (estimating)	high-frequency words; language arts words; math words; academic words	spelling patterns -*ame*, -*ate*, -*eat*, -*ing*, -*age*, -*net*; word ending -*ing*;

30	grow, together, thought, between, sentence, summarize, example, answer (solutions)	high-frequency words; language arts words; academic words	spelling patterns -it, -out, -oil, -ool, -ot; -s ending; consonant blends
31	young, laugh, family, children, infection, parasite, prescribe, physical (antibiotics)	high-frequency words; science/health words	spelling patterns -at, -oat, -ic; word parts bio, anti; prefix pre-; word parts para, scrib; suffix -tion; ph with /f/ sound; endings -el, -le, -al with same sound
32	inside, watch, somewhere, subset, frequency, integer, infinite, coordinates (submarine)	high-frequency words; math words	spelling patterns -an, -ain, -ean, -ear, -are; prefixes sub-, co-, in-; compound words; homophones
33	without, sometimes, coast, mountains, highlands, erosion, conservation, prairie (weathering)	high-frequency words; science words; social studies words	spelling patterns -eat, -ear, -ight, -eight; compound words; prefix re-; suffixes -sion, -tion, -ing; homophones
34	strong, other, folktale, animal, eclipse, gravity, fossil, discovery (dinosaurs)	high-frequency words; science words; language arts words	spelling patterns -ain, -ound, -our, -aid, -and, -od; prefix dis-; -y ending
35	might, already, let's, skeleton, digestion, stomach, circulation, heart (skeletons)	high-frequency words; science words	spelling patterns -oss, -ot, eek, -one; suffix -tion; plurals; kn where k is silent; blends sl- and st-; difference between all ready and already; apostrophe

(*Words in parentheses are the mystery words in the Day 3: Word Builder activity.*)

Systematic Word Study for Grades 2–3 © 2011 by Cheryl M. Sigmon, Scholastic Teaching Resources

The How-To's of the Five-Day Weekly Activities

Here are the directions and materials for each activity included in your weekly offerings:

Day 1: Meet the Words

Materials: For each student: seal-top plastic bag, a copy of the word template for the lesson. Cut the word template as shown below for distribution.

- Depending upon the sharpness of your scissors, you can cut 4–6 copies of the word template at the same time. Put copies of the template together. Then, along the horizontal dashed line, cut off the bottom strip of letters. Reserve the letter strip for the Day 3: Word Builder activity.

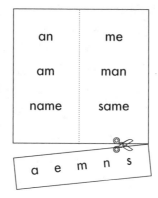

- Fold the copies of the template along the dashed vertical line so the words are visible.

- From the outside edge, cut toward the fold and stop within a half-inch of it. Do this for each of the words.

- Unfold the templates, keeping them together. From the bottom, cut along the dashed vertical line to within one inch of the top.

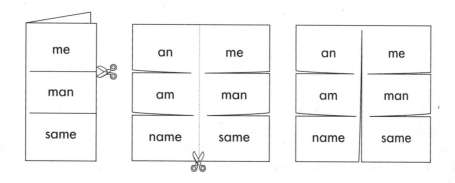

- The templates resemble a rib cage and will stay intact as you pass them out to students.

- Place a set of the week's words and letters in a plastic bag for each student. You can use a permanent marker to write each student's name on a bag. The bags don't have to be labeled since they contain the same set of words and letters, but doing so can help avoid squabbles later.

- At the end of the activity, have students return their word cards to the plastic bag.

Directions: Direct students to detach the 8 words on the template by pulling them apart. Encourage them not to attempt to tear with perfection as you want this task accomplished quickly. Then have students spread the 8 word cards across the top of their desk or table with the words faceup so that each word is visible. This will give them a generous work space and will keep little elbows from knocking the words to the floor as they work.

You will be sharing information about features of the words—plurals, double consonants, silent letters, hidden words, and so on—as well as definitions and the relationships among the words.

As you guide the students through the lessons, you can easily offer appropriate support to differentiate the activity in a number of ways, such as the following:

- Ask students needing help to work alongside a partner who can support them. However, encourage all students to manipulate their own letter and word cards so that they stay engaged rather than becoming passive participants.

- Move in close proximity to students who need assistance so that you can guide them to think about choices they are making.

- Give students permission to look at classmates' choices if they need help.

Day 2: Word Whittle/Stump the Class

(**Note:** If you don't have time to do both activities on the same day, you can choose one and save the other for another day or you can rotate between the two activities weekly. Stump the Class can also be a meaningful and challenging homework assignment.)

Word Whittle

Materials: lesson word cards

Directions: Ask students to take the words from the plastic bag and spread them across the top of their desk or table so there is adequate workspace below. For each set of the three or four questions, you are asking students to use the answers to "whittle" down the words until only one word remains. After students select the words to answer the first

Systematic Word Study for Grades 2–3 © 2011 by Cheryl M. Sigmon, Scholastic Teaching Resources

question in the set, *they cannot add any other words to that group*. At the beginning of each set of four questions, students should make sure that all 8 word cards are arranged at the top of the desk or table.

Stump the Class

Materials: lesson word cards; a Word Clusters reproducible (page 127) for each pair or small group, one transparency (optional)

Directions: Students work together to find ways to sort the words into categories of their choice. The categories can focus on any characteristic—semantic, syntactical, a configuration, or any relationship they see among any of the week's words. Students don't have to use all 8 words, and they can use the words more than one time. They should look at the words, search for a characteristic that some of the words share, copy those words into one of the circles on the Word Clusters reproducible, and then write the category underneath the words, in the rectangle. Challenge students to find unique categories that will stump the rest of the class when individuals or groups present their cluster of words. Once students have had time to create several word clusters, have each pair or group write their words—but not the category—in a circle on the board or on a transparency. The rest of the class should try to guess the category. Even though the guesses may identify a valid relationship among the words, the only correct answer for this activity is the one selected by the pair or group presenting it.

(**Note:** If you do this with an electronic whiteboard, you might write all 8 words in the box on the Word Clusters reproducible. Each time students in the pair or group share their words, they can use their fingers to drag the words into the circle, which takes far less time than having them write the words.)

You can also assign this activity for homework. Have students write the 8 words in the box on the Word Clusters reproducible. At home, they should group the words and fill in the categories. The next day, as time allows, students can try to stump the class with their word clusters.

Day 3: Word Builder

Materials: letter strips detached from the word template on Day 1; you may either cut the letters apart and distribute them to students or hand out the strips and have students tear apart the letters carefully

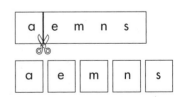

Directions: Ask students to arrange their set of letters across their desks. To help students become more familiar with the alphabet, encourage them to place the letters in alphabetical order.

Start with the first column of words. Call out each word in the sequence in which it appears and have students spell it. The words are sequenced so that they build upon letters and patterns. Omit any words that you feel are inappropriate for your students. Offer assistance as necessary with directions such as the following:

Use 3 letters to spell use.

Keep all the letters in stop. *Rearrange them to spell* spot.

Change only the first letter in pin *to spell* tin.

Add a letter at the beginning of hen *to spell* then.

After students spell the word, write it on the board or on an index card and display it in a pocket chart to allow them to cross-check their spelling. You may want to place words with the same spelling patterns together at this time, or you may wait until all words have been given before you have the students help you sort them by word patterns.

The last word you call out will be the mystery word, which uses all of the letters. Before students spell the mystery word, reveal the clue in the lesson to challenge them to figure out what the big word is and to spell it without your saying the word first.

Then begin sorting the words. Place them in rows based on their spelling patterns so that students clearly see the similarity in their spellings. Emphasize that spelling patterns help us spell many additional words. After sorting, point out the additional word features provided in the lesson, such as beginning clusters, prefixes, plural endings, and superlatives. *Note*: Sorting can extend into the Day 4: Rhymer activity or be done solely with that activity.

Day 4: Rhymer

Return to some of the spelling patterns from your Day 3: Word Builder activity. There will often be too many patterns to use in this activity, so be sure to choose the words that will give your students the greatest opportunities to make new words. Together, brainstorm a list of words that can be spelled using these patterns. This can be done in one of the following ways:

- Brainstorm with the whole group and make a list of words that can be spelled using these patterns.

- Assign the same or different patterns to partners or small groups. Have them create a list of words to share with the class.

- Make the small-group assignment competitive. Display a spelling pattern and let each group take turns adding a word until only one group can think of a word to add. You might want groups to use a dictionary to verify their words to help develop their dictionary skills.

Systematic Word Study for Grades 2–3 © 2011 by Cheryl M. Sigmon, Scholastic Teaching Resources

Day 5: Word Smart

Materials: lesson word cards

Directions: Ask students to spread the 8 lesson words across the top of their desk or table with the words visible. This will provide generous workspace for them and keep little elbows from knocking the word cards to the floor as they work. As you pose the riddles, students respond in one of the following ways:

1. Search for the answer among the 8 word cards. Pick up the word card that answers the riddle and hold it for the teacher to see. If there are more than two correct answers, choose only two answers. (Keep a watchful eye on students who consistently rely on neighbors for answers. You may need to stand in close proximity to coach them.)

2. Search for the answers among the 8 word cards. Pick the word card or cards that answer the riddle and put them in the workspace. (Randomly check their work as you monitor the room.)

Ask the riddles and affirm responses. Praise their efforts liberally!

Maximizing the Impact of Your Lessons

Here are some hints that will help you make the most of these lessons:

- Be sure that *every* student participates in these lessons. All students should have the opportunity to manipulate their own letters and words in response to your guidance. Remember that the lessons are multilevel in order to address the individual needs of a range of achievement levels. So, when some students struggle a bit with parts of a lesson, be sure to offer the support they need to be successful.

- All teachers have to deal with short weeks from time to time, so below we provide a recommended plan for the number of days you might have.

3-Day Plan

Day 1: Meet the Words
(Assign Stump the Class as homework by giving students the Word Clusters reproducible on page 127.)

Day 2: Word Builder
(Assign Rhymer as homework by giving students three or four of the patterns from the

Word Builder activity to find new words that can be spelled with those patterns. Ask them to verify spellings in the dictionary and bring in words and spellings the next day.)

Day 3: Word Smart with homework (Send home the Parent-Child Word Work reproducible, page 128.)

4-Day Plan

Day 1: Meet the Words

Day 2: Word Whittle and Stump the Class

Day 3: Word Builder with Rhymer as homework

Day 4: Word Smart with homework (Parent-Child Word Work reproducible, page 128)

- Involve parents in this word study plan. Take advantage of open-house nights or conferences to explain how they can support your efforts in building their child's word knowledge. At the conclusion of the weekly activities, send home the seal-top plastic bag of letters and words that you've used during the week. Include a Word Work homework activity sheet. Be sure to fill in the blanks with spelling patterns from the week. Everything else on the sheet will be completed by the parents/students.

- Briskly pace all the activities in your weekly plan. Reassure students who are struggling that they'll soon catch up. The activities are constructed to be multileveled so that they are appropriate for low-achieving, average, and high-achieving students. For example, Word Builder starts with simple two-letter words and works up to the mystery word, which is usually multisyllabic. Not all students will be able to build the mystery word before they see you write it.

- Go beyond these lessons with your instruction and exploration. You must still teach vocabulary in your reading and content lessons; however, as your students analyze the words through these systematic lessons, they should develop word savvy that transfers as they encounter the words in other contexts.

- Reinforce the words in these lessons at every opportunity. Repetition throughout the year is what will cause the words to truly become "known words." Here are some ideas for achieving that:

  - Point out the words during reading lessons.

  - Encourage correct use of the words in students' writings.

  - Post the high-frequency words on a word wall in the classroom and the content words on cluster charts by subject.

  - Make other teachers aware of the words that you consider critical for students' growth.

 Systematic Word Study for Grades 2–3 © 2011 by Cheryl M. Sigmon, Scholastic Teaching Resources

- With the occasional spare time that occurs in a classroom, review the week's words or review words from some of the previous weeks.

Above all else, have fun with this systematic plan for developing the vocabulary and word knowledge of your students!

Bibliography

The American Heritage dictionary of the English language. (2006). Boston: Houghton Mifflin Harcourt.

Bromley, K. (2007). Nine things every teacher should know about words and vocabulary instruction. *Journal of Adolescent & Adult Literacy, 50*(7), 528–537.

Fry, E., & Kress, J. (2006). *The reading teacher's book of lists* (5th ed.). San Francisco: Jossey-Bass.

Lehr, F., Osborne, J., & Hiebert, E. (2004). *A focus on vocabulary (Research-Based Practices in Early Reading)*. Honolulu, HI: Pacific Resources for Education and Learning.

Mountain, L. (2005, May). ROOTing out meaning: More morphemic analysis for primary pupils. *The Reading Teacher, 58*(8), 742–749.

Sigmon, C. (2007). *Just-right comprehension mini-lessons: Grades 2–3*. New York: Scholastic Teaching Resources.

Torgesen, J. K., Rashotte, C. A., & Alexander, A. W. (2001). Principles of fluency instruction in reading: Relationships with established empirical outcomes. In M. Wolf (Ed.). *Dyslexia, fluency, and the brain.* (pp. 333–355) Austin, TX: Pro-Ed.

Zeno, S. M., Ivens, S. H., Millard, R. T., & Duvvuri, R. (1995). *The educator's word frequency guide*. Brewster, NY: Touchstone Applied Science Associates.

Recommended Web Sites

www.dictionary.com

www.rhymer.com

www.wordsmith.org

Day 1: Meet the Words

Have students pull apart the 8 word cards for this lesson and arrange the cards across the top of their desk. Then ask them to do the following:

- Hold up each card as you pronounce the word on it.
- Look at the word, read it aloud, and spell it with you.
- Return the word card to the top of their desk.

Say each word. Provide a simple definition as necessary and share some of its features as described below. You may want to have students use their fingers to cover certain letters to isolate phonic elements such as initial letters, blends, vowels, or hidden words, or point to certain letters as you discuss them. Clap the syllables in each word, and use it in a sentence that helps students understand the meaning of the word.

Some notable features of these words include the following:

✳ **been**: frequently-used word; verb; double *e* does not have long-*e* sound like *sheep, sleep*; hidden words: *be, bee*

✳ **off**: frequently-used word; preposition; opposite of *on*; one *f* difference from *of*; hidden word: *of*

✳ **cold**: frequently-used word; adjective; opposite of *hot*; spelling pattern helps spell words like *old, fold, mold, bold*; hidden word: *old*

✳ **tell**: frequently-used word; verb; -*ell* says letter name for *l*; spelling pattern helps spell words like *bell, fell, dell, Nell, sell*

✳ **publish**: verb; stage of writing process after revision and editing when the piece is ready for others to see: Writing can be published in different forms—books, newspapers, on wall of classroom, etc.

✳ **unknown**: adjective; prefix *un-* means "not"; unknown means "not known or unfamiliar"; hidden words: *know, no, now, known, own*

✳ **unlikely**: adverb; prefix *un-* means "not"; compare to *unknown*; means "not likely or not probable"; hidden words: *like, likely*

✳ **interpret**: verb; in science, means "to study something read or observed and to give your point of view of what it means"; another meaning involves changing one language into another, such as interpreting Spanish into English or spoken words into visual words; hidden word: *in*

Day 2: Word Whittle

Distribute the plastic bags containing this week's words or ask students to retrieve them. Have students place the words across the top of their workspace. After you read the first clue, they pull down all the words that fit it. For each subsequent clue in the set, students continue to whittle the words by returning those that don't fit to the top of their workspace. No new words can be added to the group after the first clue. Only one word will remain after the final clue in a set. Students return the word card to the top of their workspace before the next set of clues begins.

First Set:
1. a word that starts with a consonant (*been, cold, tell, publish*)
2. a word that is a verb (*been, tell, publish*)
3. a word that has at least one tall letter (*been, tell, publish*)
4. a word that rhymes with the name of something that lets us know school is out (*tell*)

Second Set:
1. a word that has 2 of the same letters (*been, off, tell, interpret, unknown*)
2. a word that starts with a consonant (*been, tell*)
3. a word that fits in this sentence: "We have _____ studying hard this year." (*been*)

Third Set:
1. a word that is a verb (*been, tell, publish, interpret*)
2. a word that has a letter that goes below the line (*publish, interpret*)
3. a word that has 3 syllables (*interpret*)

Fourth Set:
1. a word that has more than 1 syllable (*publish, interpret, unlikely, unknown*)
2. a word that starts with a prefix (*unlikely, unknown*)
3. a word that starts with a prefix that means "not" (*unlikely, unknown*)
4. a word that is a synonym for *unfamiliar* (*unknown*)

Stump the Class

Give pairs or small groups time to work together to find relationships among this week's words. Once they have found a category into which several of the words fit, they should write the words in a circle on the Word Clusters sheet (see page 127) and the category underneath. Allow time for each pair or group to share one set of their words and ask the rest of the class to guess the category. Even though the other students may suggest a legitimate category, only the presenters' category is the correct answer. The goal is to stump the rest of the class with a unique category. (You might discover categories that you can add to the Day 5: Word Smart activity.)

Day 3: Word Builder

Have students separate the letters at the bottom of this week's word template. Ask them to spell words as you call them out. Have students construct words based on patterns in the words and call out words in increasingly difficult order as shown below. The final word should answer this clue: They helped us get all of the books we have. (*publishers*)

rush	blue	blur	sip	help
bush	bluish	slur	slip	publish
blush	hub	slurp	lip	publisher
brush	rub		lips	publishers
	shrub			

As students spell each word, write it on the board. Ask them to cross-check their spelling with yours and correct any errors. On the board or in a pocket chart, sort the words according to the following spelling patterns:

-ush	-ub	-ur	-ip
rush	hub	blur	sip
bush	rub	slur	slip
blush	shrub		lip
brush			

After all the words have been spelled and sorted, have students read over the list, emphasizing the spelling pattern from the first vowel to the end of each word. In the case of multisyllabic words, the rimes are a bit different, so stress the rhymes of these words.

Tell students that these patterns can help them spell many other words. The Day 4 activity will start with these patterns.

Take an opportunity to talk about some of the following elements: consonant blends (*shr-, bl-, -sh, sl-*); suffixes (*publisher, publishers, lips*); plurals (*publishers, lips*).

Day 4: Rhymer

Return to some of the patterns from the Day 3 lesson. With students, brainstorm a list of words using these rime patterns. This can be done in several different ways:

- The whole group brainstorms with you and makes a list.
- Assign the same or different patterns to partners or small groups. Have them create a list of words to share with the class.
- Make the small-group assignment competitive. Choose a pattern and let each group take turns adding a word to the list until only one group is able to add a word. You might want to let groups use a dictionary to verify their words.

Day 5: Word Smart

Distribute the Lesson 1 words and ask students to arrange them across the top of their desk with plenty of workspace below. Have students respond to your questions by picking up the correct word card(s) and holding it so you can see their answer. If there are more than two correct answers, tell students to show only two—one in each hand. Ask students, "Can you find the . . ."

- word hiding the word *old*?
- word hiding the word *now*?
- word that names the part of the writing process when a piece of writing is ready to show others?
- word that is the opposite of *on*?
- word that is the opposite of *hot*?
- word that has a prefix that means "not"?
- word that is an adjective?
- word that is a verb?
- word hiding two words that are pronounced "no" but are spelled 2 different ways?
- word that starts the same way as *international*?
- word with a prefix that rhymes with *bun*?
- word with 3 syllables?
- word that ends the same way as the word *stylish*?
- word that fits in this sentence: "Without our star player, it is _____ that we will win the game."?
- word hiding a little word that says something belongs to someone?
- word that describes what you do when you watch or read something and then tell what you feel it means?
- word with a word part that means the opposite of *out*?
- word with double consonants?
- word with 2 syllables?
- word that means changing one language into another?

✳ Homework ✳

After Day 5, words go home with students. They review the words and use them to complete the Parent-Child Word Work page (see page 128).

Day 1: Meet the Words

Have students pull apart the 8 word cards for this lesson and arrange the cards across the top of their desk. Then ask them to do the following:

- Hold up each card as you pronounce the word on it.
- Look at the word, read it aloud, and spell it with you.
- Return the word card to the top of their desk.

Say each word. Provide a simple definition as necessary and share some of its features as described below. You may want to have students use their fingers to cover certain letters to isolate phonic elements such as initial letters, blends, vowels, or hidden words, or point to certain letters as you discuss them. Clap the syllables in each word, and use it in a sentence that helps students understand the meaning of the word.

Some notable features of these words include the following:

✳ **work**: frequently-used word; noun or verb ("Let's get our work done." "Let's work together."); beginning sound /w/ and ending sound /k/; -or makes the sound of er, ir, ur; hidden word: or

✳ **first**: frequently-used word; adjective ("He is in the first grade.") /û/ sound; transition word in reading/writing: first, next, last; 3 syllables; hidden word: fir

✳ **goes**: frequently-used word; verb; used with singular nouns and pronouns; hidden word: go

✳ **does**: frequently-used word; verb; used with singular nouns and pronouns; compare to spelling pattern of goes in which base word is distinguishable; different pronunciation is plural meaning "female deer"; hidden word: do

✳ **adjective**: word used often in language arts; describes a noun or pronoun: blue dress, first grade, rainy night, silly me, fussy baby; hidden word: ad

✳ **county**: word used often in social studies; a division of government within a state, usually comprising towns, cities, or municipalities; -y makes long-e sound; 2 syllables; hidden word: count

✳ **rural**: word used often in social studies; adjective that relates to areas outside of cities sometimes referred to as "the country" ("We like living in a rural area that doesn't have so much traffic."); 2 syllables

✳ **urban**: word used often in social studies; adjective that relates to a city or a densely populated area ("We like living in an urban area because of the stores and events nearby."); 2 syllables; hidden word: ban

Day 2: Word Whittle

Distribute the plastic bags containing this week's words or ask students to retrieve them. Have students place the words across the top of their workspace. After you read the first clue, they pull down all the words that fit it. For each subsequent clue in the set, students continue to whittle the words by returning those that don't fit to the top of their workspace. No new words can be added to the group after the first clue. Only one word will remain after the final clue in a set. Students return the word card to the top of their workspace before the next set of clues begins.

First Set:

1. a word that has 2 syllables (county, rural, urban)
2. a word that relates to locations/places (county, rural, urban)
3. a word that has a tall letter (county, rural, urban)
4. a word that is hiding a math word (county)

Second Set:

1. a word that has 1 syllable (work, first, goes, does)
2. a word that starts with a letter in the first half of the alphabet (first, goes, does)
3. a word that looks like its plural, but it isn't (goes, does)
4. a word that has a long-o sound (goes)

Third Set:

1. a word that starts with a consonant (work, first, goes, does, county, rural)
2. a word that has an o (work, goes, does, county)
3. a word that has a tall letter (work, does, county)
4. a word that refers to a region within a state that has several cities or towns (county)

Fourth Set:

1. a word that has an a (adjective, rural, urban)
2. a word that has more than 1 syllable (adjective, rural, urban)
3. a word that starts with a vowel (adjective, urban)
4. a word that describes a person, place, or thing (adjective)

Stump the Class

Give pairs or small groups time to work together to find relationships among this week's words. Once they have found a category into which several of the words fit, they should write the words in a circle on the Word Clusters sheet (see page 127) and the category underneath. Allow time for each pair or group to share one set of their words and ask the rest of the class to guess the category. Even though the other students may suggest a legitimate category, only the presenters' category is the correct answer. The goal is to stump the rest of the class with a unique category. (You might discover categories that you can add to the Day 5: Word Smart activity.)

Day 3: Word Builder

Have students separate the letters at the bottom of this week's word template. Ask them to spell words as you call them out. Have students construct words based on patterns in the words and call out words in increasingly difficult order as shown below. The final word should answer this clue: This describes an area where people might live just outside of a city. (*suburban*)

sub	ran	bar
rub	run	barn
ban	bun	bus
urn	buns	urban
burn		suburban

As students spell each word, write it on the board. Ask them to cross-check their spelling with yours and correct any errors. On the board or in a pocket chart, sort the words according to the following spelling patterns:

-ub	-urn
sub	urn
rub	burn

After all the words have been spelled and sorted, have students read over the list, emphasizing the spelling pattern from the first vowel to the end of each word. In the case of multisyllabic words, the rimes are a bit different, so stress the rhymes of these words.

Tell students that these patterns can help them spell many other words. The Day 4 activity will start with these patterns.

Take an opportunity to talk about the prefix *sub-*, which means "below." How does this meaning relate to *submarine* and *subway*?

Day 4: Rhymer

Return to some of the patterns from the Day 3 lesson. With students, brainstorm a list of words using these rime patterns. This can be done in several different ways:

- The whole group brainstorms with you and makes a list.

- Assign the same or different patterns to partners or small groups. Have them create a list of words to share with the class.

- Make the small-group assignment competitive. Choose a pattern and let each group take turns adding a word to the list until only one group is able to add a word. You might want to let groups use a dictionary to verify their words.

Day 5: Word Smart

Distribute the Lesson 2 words and ask students to arrange them across the top of their desk with plenty of workspace below. Have students respond to your questions by picking up the correct word card(s) and holding it so you can see their answer. If there are more than two correct answers, tell students to show only two—one in each hand. Ask students, "Can you find the . . ."

- word hiding a word that is the opposite of *stop*?

- word that ends the way the word *stay* begins?

- word with 3 syllables?

- word that fits in this sentence: "His farm was in a beautiful _____ area of the country."?

- word that fits in this sentence: "The _____ area had many theaters, shops, and grocery stores."?

- word hiding a math word?

- word that starts with a vowel?

- word that starts the same way the word *fire* does?

- word that names the part of speech that includes the words *pretty, purple, old,* and *smooth*?

- words that are spelled the same way except for one letter?

- word that has the same last syllable as *pretty*?

- word that combined with the word *home* describes something you have to do at home?

- word whose second syllable has the beginning letter of *jungle*?

- word hiding the name of a type of tree?

- word hiding something we see on TV or in newspapers?

- word that ends the same way the word *break* ends?

- words whose endings are spelled the same but have different sounds?

- word hiding a word that means "to forbid something"?

✳ Homework ✳

After Day 5, words go home with students. They review the words and use them to complete the Parent-Child Word Work page (see page 128).

Day 1: Meet the Words

Have students pull apart the 8 word cards for this lesson and arrange the cards across the top of their desk. Then ask them to do the following:

- Hold up each card as you pronounce the word on it.
- Look at the word, read it aloud, and spell it with you.
- Return the word card to the top of their desk.

Say each word. Provide a simple definition as necessary and share some of its features as described below. You may want to have students use their fingers to cover certain letters to isolate phonic elements such as initial letters, blends, vowels, or hidden words, or point to certain letters as you discuss them. Clap the syllables in each word, and use it in a sentence that helps students understand the meaning of the word.

Some notable features of these words include the following:

✳ **them**: frequently-used word; pronoun; hidden words: *he, hem, the*

✳ **your**: frequently-used word; possessive pronoun (shows ownership); hidden word: *our*

✳ **their**: frequently-used word; possessive pronoun (shows ownership); hidden words: *the, heir, he*

✳ **pronoun**: word used often in language arts; means "a word that takes the place of a noun"—e.g., *he, she, it, they, them, we, us*; 2 syllables; hidden words: *noun, pro, no*

✳ **us**: frequently-used word; pronoun; spelling pattern *-us* helps spell words like *bus* and *pus*

✳ **compare**: academic word, often used in language arts; means "to look at similarities between or among items"; 2 syllables; hidden words: *pa, pare, are*

✳ **contrast**: academic word, often used in language arts; means "to look at the differences between or among items"; 2 syllables; hidden words: *con, on*

✳ **dissolve**: word used often in science; means "to make a solution or mixture"; double consonant *s*; 2 syllables; hidden words: *solve, so, is*

Day 2: Word Whittle

Distribute the plastic bags containing this week's words or ask students to retrieve them. Have students place the words across the top of their workspace. After you read the first clue, they pull down all the words that fit it. For each subsequent clue in the set, students continue to whittle the words by returning those that don't fit to the top of their workspace. No new words can be added to the group after the first clue. Only one word will remain after the final clue in a set. Students return the word card to the top of their workspace before the next set of clues begins.

First Set:

1. a word that is a pronoun (*them, your, their, us*)
2. a word that has a /th/ sound (*them, their*)
3. a pronoun that refers to more than 1 person (*them, their*)
4. a pronoun that shows ownership—that something belongs to someone (*their*)

Second Set:

1. a word that has 2 syllables (*pronoun, compare, contrast, dissolve*)
2. a word that has 3 vowels (*pronoun, compare, dissolve*)
3. a word that has letters below the line (*pronoun, compare*)
4. a word that means "looking at the similarities between 2 or more things" (*compare*)

Third Set:

1. a word that has fewer than 6 letters (*them, your, their, us*)
2. a word that is a pronoun (*them, your, their, us*)
3. a word that has tall letters (*them, their*)
4. a word that fits in this sentence: "Do you want to go to lunch with _____?" (*them*)

Fourth Set:

1. a word that starts and ends with a consonant (*them, your, their, pronoun, contrast*)
2. a word that has an *r* (*your, their, pronoun, contrast*)
3. a word that has 2 syllables (*pronoun, contrast*)
4. a word that rhymes with *fast* (*contrast*)

Stump the Class

Give pairs or small groups time to work together to find relationships among this week's words. Once they have found a category into which several of the words fit, they should write the words in a circle on the Word Clusters sheet (see page 127) and the category underneath. Allow time for each pair or group to share one set of their words and ask the rest of the class to guess the category. Even though the other students may suggest a legitimate

category, only the presenters' category is the correct answer. The goal is to stump the rest of the class with a unique category. (You might discover categories that you can add to the Day 5: Word Smart activity.)

Day 3: Word Builder

Have students separate the letters at the bottom of this week's word template. Ask them to spell words as you call them out. Have students construct words based on patterns in the words and call out words in increasingly difficult order as shown below. The final word should answer this clue: When we compare items, we find this. (*similarities*)

rail	sis	sir	time
sail	sister	stir	timer
mail	slim	mist	limits
male	stem	mister	similar
sale	mile		similarities
	smile		

As students spell each word, write it on the board. Ask them to cross-check their spelling with yours and correct any errors. On the board or in a pocket chart, sort the words according to the following spelling patterns:

-ail	-ale	-ir
rail	male	sir
sail	sale	stir
mail		

After all the words have been spelled and sorted, have students read over the list, emphasizing the spelling pattern from the first vowel to the end of each word. In the case of multisyllabic words, the rimes are a bit different, so stress the rhymes of these words.

Tell students that these patterns can help them spell many other words. The Day 4 activity will start with these patterns.

Take an opportunity to talk about some of the following elements: homophones (*sale/sail*); suffixes (*-er*).

Day 4: Rhymer

Return to some of the patterns from the Day 3 lesson. With students, brainstorm a list of words using these rime patterns. This can be done in several different ways:

- The whole group brainstorms with you and makes a list.
- Assign the same or different patterns to partners or small groups. Have them create a list of words to share with the class.
- Make the small-group assignment competitive. Choose a pattern and let each group take turns adding a word to the list

until only one group is able to add a word. You might want to let groups use a dictionary to verify their words.

Day 5: Word Smart

Distribute the Lesson 3 words and ask students to arrange them across the top of their desk with plenty of workspace below. Have students respond to your questions by picking up the correct word card(s) and holding it so you can see their answer. If there are more than two correct answers, tell students to show only two—one in each hand. Ask students, "Can you find the . . ."

- word that is a pronoun showing ownership?
- word that is a pronoun referring to more than 1 person?
- word that rhymes with *bus*?
- word hiding what you do to math problems?
- word hiding a pronoun?
- word that has 2 syllables?
- word that starts like the word *promote*?
- word that starts like the word *complete*?
- word that rhymes with *touchdown*?
- words that rhyme with each other even though they have different spelling patterns?
- words that fit in this sentence: "We are going to _____ and _____ these two characters from our story."?
- word that rhymes with *revolve*?
- word that is the longest in this lesson?
- word that is the shortest in this lesson?
- word that takes the place of a noun?
- word hiding someone who is paid for playing a sport?
- word that rhymes with *sportscast*?
- word that refers to similarities?
- word that refers to differences?

❄ Homework ❄

After Day 5, words go home with students. They review the words and use them to complete the Parent-Child Word Work page (see page 128).

Day 1: Meet the Words

Have students pull apart the 8 word cards for this lesson and arrange the cards across the top of their desk. Then ask them to do the following:

- Hold up each card as you pronounce the word on it.
- Look at the word, read it aloud, and spell it with you.
- Return the word card to the top of their desk.

Say each word. Provide a simple definition as necessary and share some of its features as described below. You may want to have students use their fingers to cover certain letters to isolate phonic elements such as initial letters, blends, vowels, or hidden words, or point to certain letters as you discuss them. Clap the syllables in each word, and use it in a sentence that helps students understand the meaning of the word.

Some notable features of these words include the following:

* **its**: frequently-used word; short-*i* beginning sound; rhymes with *bits, pits, fits*, although with those words the -*s* makes them plural; in *its*, the -*s* shows that something belongs to it, as in "The dog is chasing its tail." (*the tail that belongs to the dog*) Or, "The class is changing its lunchtime." (*the lunchtime that belongs to the class*); the word *it's* is different because of its apostrophe: *it's* is a contraction for *it is* ("It's time to go to lunch.")

* **around**: frequently-used word; 2 syllables; /ou/ sound; listen carefully to the ending /n/ /d/; used often as a preposition, like the words *up, down, under*; pattern helps to spell *found, sound, bound*; hidden words: *a, round*

* **don't**: frequently-used word; contraction that means "do not"; apostrophe used for the omitted letter; we use contractions in our everyday conversations in written and spoken language; hidden words: *do, on*

* **right**: frequently-used word; rhymes with *kite* but has a different spelling pattern (-*ite* and -*ight* both "say" the same thing); long-*i* sound; *write/right* are homophones—same pronunciation but different spellings and meanings; *right* means "correct," as in "All of his math problems were right."

* **plural**: word used often in language arts; means "more than one of something"; often the suffix -*s* or -*es* is a signal that something is plural: *bird-birds, dog-dogs, boy-boys, girl-girls, fox-foxes*; some plurals are different: *mouse-mice, goose-geese*; 2 syllables; beginning /pl/ sound

* **fraction**: word used often in math; means "a part of something or less than a whole" ("I could only eat a fraction of the pizza." "We are only a fraction of the way there."); 2 syllables; hidden words: *act, action, on*

* **one-fourth**: word often used in math; a number that is a fraction; the first part (*one*) shows how many parts of the whole; the second part (*fourth*) tells how many parts the whole is divided into; one-fourth of a pizza would look like (*draw this*); mark between the 2 words is a hyphen linking the words; 2 syllables; hidden words: *one, fourth, on, our, four*

* **one-third**: word often used in math; a number that is a fraction; *one* tells how many parts of the whole; *third* tells us there are 3 parts in the whole; one-third of a pizza would look like (*draw*); 2 syllables; hidden words: *one, third, on*

Day 2: Word Whittle

Distribute the plastic bags containing this week's words or ask students to retrieve them. Have students place the words across the top of their workspace. After you read the first clue, they pull down all the words that fit it. For each subsequent clue in the set, students continue to whittle the words by returning those that don't fit to the top of their workspace. No new words can be added to the group after the first clue. Only one word will remain after the final clue in a set. Students return the word card to the top of their workspace before the next set of clues begins.

First Set:
1. a word that has an *i* (*its, right, fraction, one-third*)
2. a word that has a *t* (*its, right, fraction, one-third*)
3. a word that has 2 syllables (*fraction, one-third*)
4. a word that means "1 out of 3 parts of something" (*one-third*)

Second Set:
1. a word that starts with a vowel (*its, around, one-fourth, one-third*)
2. a word that has at least 1 tall letter (*its, around, one-fourth, one-third*)
3. a word that has a hyphen (*one-fourth, one-third*)
4. a word that means "1 out of 4 parts of something" (*one-fourth*)

Third Set:
1. a word that has 2 syllables (*around, plural, fraction, one-fourth, one-third*)
2. a word that has an *a* (*around, plural, fraction*)
3. a word that starts with a consonant (*plural, fraction*)
4. a word that means "more than one" (*plural*)

Fourth Set:
1. a word that ends with a tall letter (*around, don't, right, plural, one-fourth, one-third*)
2. a word that starts and ends with a consonant (*don't, right, plural*)
3. a word with a vowel as its second letter (*don't, right*)
4. a word that is a contraction (*don't*)

Stump the Class

Give pairs or small groups time to work together to find relationships among this week's words. Once they have found a category into which several of the words fit, they should write the words in a circle on the Word Clusters sheet (see page 127) and the category underneath. Allow time for each pair or group to share one set of their words and ask the rest of the class to guess the category. Even though the other students may suggest a legitimate category, only the presenters' category is the correct answer. The goal is to stump the rest of the class with a unique category. (You might discover categories that you can add to the Day 5: Word Smart activity.)

Day 3: Word Builder

Have students separate the letters at the bottom of this week's word template. Ask them to spell words as you call them out. Have students construct words based on patterns in the words and call out words in increasingly difficult order as shown below. The final word should answer this clue: When we don't have a whole, we have this. (*fractions*)

can	art	cost	acorn	first
tan	act	frost	far	sift
scan	fact	front	fin	sonic
at	corn	raft	fit	scarf
rat	scorn	craft	fist	fractions

As students spell each word, write it on the board. Ask them to cross-check their spelling with yours and correct any errors. On the board or in a pocket chart, sort the words according to the following spelling patterns:

-an	-at	-act	-orn	-ost	-aft
can	at	act	corn	cost	raft
tan	rat	fact	scorn	frost	craft
scan			acorn		

After all the words have been spelled and sorted, have students read over the list, emphasizing the spelling pattern from the first vowel to the end of each word. In the case of multisyllabic words, the rimes are a bit different, so stress the rhymes of these words.

Tell students that these patterns can help them spell many other words. The Day 4 activity will start with these patterns.

Take an opportunity to talk about some of the following elements: consonant blends (*sc-: scarf, scan, scorn; fr-: frost, front, fractions; -st: first, frost*).

Day 4: Rhymer

Return to some of the patterns from the Day 3 lesson. With

students, brainstorm a list of words using these rime patterns. This can be done in several different ways:

- The whole group brainstorms with you and makes a list.
- Assign the same or different patterns to partners or small groups. Have them create a list of words to share with the class.
- Make the small-group assignment competitive. Choose a pattern and let each group take turns adding a word to the list until only one group is able to add a word. You might want to let groups use a dictionary to verify their words.

Day 5: Word Smart

Distribute the Lesson 4 words and ask students to arrange them across the top of their desk with plenty of workspace below. Have students respond to your questions by picking up the correct word card(s) and holding it so you can see their answer. If there are more than two correct answers, tell students to show only two—one in each hand. Ask students, "Can you find the . . ."

- word that means "more than one of something"?
- word that fits in this sentence: "I could only eat _____ of the pizza."?
- word that starts with a vowel?
- word that is the shortest in this lesson? longest?
- word that is the opposite of *wrong*?
- word that is a contraction?
- words hiding the word *round*? *act*? *four*? *do*?
- word that means "do not"?
- word that means "a part of something"?
- word that shows possession?
- word that fits in this sentence: "You'll have to go _____ the building to find the playground."?
- word that means "one of 4 parts"? "one of 3 parts"?
- word with an apostrophe? a hyphen?
- word hiding the word *action*?
- word that starts the same way as the words *French fry*?
- word that rhymes with *bright*? *found*?
- word that begins like *please* does?

Day 1: Meet the Words

Have students pull apart the 8 word cards for this lesson and arrange the cards across the top of their desk. Then ask them to do the following:

- Hold up each card as you pronounce the word on it.
- Look at the word, read it aloud, and spell it with you.
- Return the word card to the top of their desk.

Say each word. Provide a simple definition as necessary and share some of its features as described below. You may want to have students use their fingers to cover certain letters to isolate phonic elements such as initial letters, blends, vowels, or hidden words, or point to certain letters as you discuss them. Clap the syllables in each word, and use it in a sentence that helps students understand the meaning of the word.

Some notable features of these words include the following:

* **would**: frequently-used word; /w/ beginning sound; /ŏŏ/; silent *l*; /d/ at end; same spelling and sound pattern as *should* and *could*; *wood* is a homophone—same pronunciation but different spelling and meaning

* **green**: frequently-used word; /gr/ at beginning; long *e*; double vowel; name of color made by blending blue and yellow; use spelling pattern for *screen*

* **call**: frequently-used word; /k/ sound at beginning; important because its spelling pattern is used for many words: *fall, ball, hall, mall*; hidden word: *all*

* **sleep**: frequently-used word; blend /sl/ at beginning like *slip, slope, sleet, slick*; double vowel makes long *e* as with *green*; spelling pattern for *sheep, steep, beep, jeep, keep*

* **revise**: prefix *re-* means "again"; in writing process, stage where you redo some things to improve writing—replace words with stronger words, rearrange some lines that are out of order, or find a better beginning; 2 syllables; hidden words: *rev, is*

* **conflict**: /k/ sound at beginning; listen to /fl/, short *i*, and sounds made by *c* and *t*; means "problem" (synonym); almost every story has a conflict or problem that needs to be solved; 2 syllables; hidden words: *con, on*

* **landmark**: compound word—two words put together to make one word: *land + mark*; in social studies, a landmark is a famous place, such as the Statue of Liberty or Mt. Rushmore, or it can refer to a recognizable place used when giving directions—a certain restaurant or gas station; both words have spelling patterns that help you spell many other words: *-and* for words like *hand, band, sand, strand*, and *-ark* for words such as *dark, park, bark, lark*; hidden words: *and, an, mar*

* **symbol**: *y* makes a short-*i* sound; one kind of symbol is something that stands for or represents something else, such as the Statue of Liberty standing for freedom, or the eagle on America's national emblem standing for bravery; another kind of symbol might be one used in a math problem (+ means "plus," = stands for "equals"); symbols also appear on signs, such as a cell phone with a line through it to indicate that cell phone use is not permitted (*list others that students think of*); *cymbal*, a band instrument that makes a loud, crashing sound, is a homophone—same pronunciation but different spelling and different meaning

Day 2: Word Whittle

Distribute the plastic bags containing this week's words or ask students to retrieve them. Have students place the words across the top of their workspace. After you read the first clue, they pull down all the words that fit it. For each subsequent clue in the set, students continue to whittle the words by returning those that don't fit to the top of their workspace. No new words can be added to the group after the first clue. Only one word will remain after the final clue in a set. Students return the word card to the top of their workspace before the next set of clues begins.

First Set:
1. a word that has 2 of the same letters (*green, call, sleep, revise, conflict, landmark*)
2. a word that has 2 of the same vowels (*green, sleep, revise, landmark*)
3. a word that has 2 vowels together (*green, sleep*)
4. a word that can help you spell the word *steep* (*sleep*)

Second Set:
1. a word that begins and ends with a consonant (*would, green, call, sleep, conflict, landmark, symbol*)
2. a word that has 2 syllables. (*revise, conflict, landmark, symbol*)
3. a word that has 3 tall letters (*conflict, landmark*)
4. a word that is a compound word (*landmark*)

Third Set:
1. a word that is a verb (*would, call, sleep, revise*)
2. a word that has an *l* (*would, call, sleep*)
3. a word that has 2 of the same letters together (*call, sleep*)
4. a word that fits in this sentence: "If you want me to help, just _____ me." (*call*)

Fourth Set:
1. a word that has an *e* (*green, sleep, revise*)
2. a word that has 2 *e*'s (*green, sleep, revise*)
3. a word that means "to change or rewrite to make a piece better" (*revise*)

Stump the Class

Give pairs or small groups time to work together to find relationships among this week's words. Once they have found a category into which several of the words fit, they should write the words in a circle on the Word Clusters sheet (see page 127) and the category underneath. Allow time for each pair or group to share one set of their words and ask the rest of the class to guess the category. Even though the other students may suggest a legitimate category, only the presenters' category is the correct answer. The goal is to stump the rest of the class with a unique category. (You might discover categories that you can add to the Day 5: Word Smart activity.)

Day 3: Word Builder

Have students separate the letters at the bottom of this week's word template. Ask them to spell words as you call them out. Have students construct words based on patterns in the words and call out words in increasingly difficult order as shown below. The final word should answer this clue: This is a landmark you would look up to. (*skyscraper*)

sack	care	ark	rap	sky
pack	scare	park	scrap	skyscraper
rack	scary	spark	scrape	
car			scraper	
scar				

As students spell each word, write it on the board. Ask them to cross-check their spelling with yours and correct any errors. On the board or in a pocket chart, sort the words according to the following spelling patterns:

-ack	-ap	-ar	-ark	-are
sack	rap	car	ark	care
pack	scrap	scar	park	scare
rack			spark	

After all the words have been spelled and sorted, have students read over the list, emphasizing the spelling pattern from the first vowel to the end of each word. In the case of multisyllabic words, the rimes are a bit different, so stress the rhymes of these words.

Tell students that these patterns can help them spell many other words. The Day 4 activity will start with these patterns.

Take an opportunity to talk about some of the following elements: long vowel/consonant/silent-*e* words (*care, scare, scrape*); compound words (*skyscraper*).

Day 4: Rhymer

Return to some of the patterns from the Day 3 lesson. With students, brainstorm a list of words using these rime patterns. This can be done in several different ways:

- The whole group brainstorms with you and makes a list.
- Assign the same or different patterns to partners or small groups. Have them create a list of words to share with the class.
- Make the small-group assignment competitive. Choose a pattern and let each group take turns adding a word to the list until only one group is able to add a word. You might want to let groups use a dictionary to verify their words.

Day 5: Word Smart

Distribute the Lesson 5 words and ask students to arrange them across the top of their desk with plenty of workspace below. Have students respond to your questions by picking up the correct word card(s) and holding it so you can see their answer. If there are more than two correct answers, tell students to show only two—one in each hand. Ask students, "Can you find the . . ."

- word that starts with a /w/ sound?
- word that starts with the same blend as the word *great*?
- word that is a compound word?
- word hiding the word *and*? *all*?
- word that, if you changed the first letter to a *b*, would name something to play with?
- word that, if you changed the second letter to a *t*, could describe a path that's hard to walk on?
- word that sounds like something you get from a tree?
- word that names a color?
- word that has 3 tall letters?
- word that rhymes with *sheep*?
- word that names something you would do after writing a story to make it better?
- word that means "a notable place," such as the Empire State Building?
- word that means "something that stands for something else"?
- word that is a synonym for *problem*?
- word that describes something you might do with a phone?
- word that names something you get when you mix blue and yellow?
- word whose first two letters mean "again"?
- word with the same spelling pattern as *could* and *should*?

✳ Homework ✳

After Day 5, words go home with students. They review the words and use them to complete the Parent-Child Word Work page (see page 128).

Day 1: Meet the Words

Have students pull apart the 8 word cards for this lesson and arrange the cards across the top of their desk. Then ask them to do the following:

- Hold up each card as you pronounce the word on it.
- Look at the word, read it aloud, and spell it with you.
- Return the word card to the top of their desk.

Say each word. Provide a simple definition as necessary and share some of its features as described below. You may want to have students use their fingers to cover certain letters to isolate phonic elements such as initial letters, blends, vowels, or hidden words, or point to certain letters as you discuss them. Clap the syllables in each word, and use it in a sentence that helps students understand the meaning of the word.

Some notable features of these words include the following:

* **five**: frequently-used word; long-*i* sound; silent *e*; spelling pattern helps spell words like *hive, jive, beehive, live*

* **wash**: frequently-used word; /w/ beginning; same spelling pattern as the following words that have a different sound: *bash, dash, mash, crash*; hidden words: *as, ash, was*

* **know**: frequently-used word; silent *k* at beginning; homophone of *no*; word part of the word *knowledge*; hidden words: *no, now*

* **before**: frequently-used word; first 2 letters *be-* combine to make the sound of the letter *b*; *fore* sounds like the number but is spelled differently; preposition, like *after, up, down, between*; silent *e* at end; 2 syllables, hidden words: *be, for*

* **edit**: 2 syllables; *edit* is what you do to clean up a piece of writing by looking for errors in spelling, punctuation, and grammar: it's the last stage of writing before publishing; hidden words: *it, Ed*

* **resource**: *re-* prefix means "again"; 2 syllables; means "something that is a source or supply": In science, there are natural resources like water, oil, wood, and sunlight; also means "something that furnishes information," such as a dictionary, thesaurus, or atlas; hidden words: *source, our, sour, so*

* **energy**: first 2 letters *en-* combine to make the sound of the letter *n*; *er* sound may be made by *er, ir, ur*; *y* makes a long-*e* sound at the end; 3 syllables; in science, energy is something that is everywhere—even though we can't see it: Energy makes things give off heat or light or makes them move. There are different types of energy—wind, water, thermal, solar, and many more. Energy also refers to the level of activity we have—high energy when we run and play or low energy when we rest.

* **nonrenewable**: 5 syllables—clap; *non-* is a prefix that means "not"; *re-* is another prefix that means "again"; suffix *-able*; In science, resources are either renewable or nonrenewable: renewable resources are those that can be replaced, such as air, water, wood, and sunlight. Some resources cannot be renewed. These nonrenewable resources include gas, oil, and coal; hidden words: *on, no, renew, able, new*

Day 2: Word Whittle

Distribute the plastic bags containing this week's words or ask students to retrieve them. Have students place the words across the top of their workspace. After you read the first clue, they pull down all the words that fit it. For each subsequent clue in the set, students continue to whittle the words by returning those that don't fit to the top of their workspace. No new words can be added to the group after the first clue. Only one word will remain after the final clue in a set. Students return the word card to the top of their workspace before the next set of clues begins.

First Set:
1. a word that has more than 1 syllable (*before, edit, resource, energy, nonrenewable*)
2. a word that has 2 syllables (*before, edit, resource*)
3. a word that has 2 *e*'s (*before, resource*)
4. a word that means "something we use to help us" (*resource*)

Second Set:
1. a word that has more than 2 syllables (*energy, nonrenewable*)
2. a word that has at least 2 *e*'s (*energy, nonrenewable*)
3. a word that might be taught in science class (*nonrenewable, energy*)
4. a word that has a prefix meaning "not" (*nonrenewable*)

Third Set:
1. a word that starts with a consonant (*five, wash, know, before, resource, nonrenewable*)
2. a word that ends with a silent *e* (*five, resource, nonrenewable*)
3. a word that has 4 or more vowels (*resource, nonrenewable*)
4. a word that means something that cannot be reused (*nonrenewable*)

Fourth Set:
1. a word that has 4 letters (*five, wash, know, edit*)
2. a word that has at least 1 tall letter (*five, wash, know, edit*)
3. a word that is not a number (*wash, know, edit*)
4. a word that is a word part of *knowledge* (*know*)

Stump the Class

Give pairs or small groups time to work together to find relationships among this week's words. Once they have found a category into which several of the words fit, they should write the words in a circle on the Word Clusters sheet (see page 127) and the category underneath. Allow time for each pair or group to share one set of their words and ask the rest of the class to guess the category. Even though the other students may suggest a legitimate category, only the presenters' category is the correct answer. The goal is to stump the rest of the class with a unique category. (You might discover categories that you can add to the Day 5: Word Smart activity.)

Day 3: Word Builder

Have students separate the letters at the bottom of this week's word template. Ask them to spell words as you call them out. Have students construct words based on patterns in the words and call out words in increasingly difficult order as shown below. The final word should answer this clue: People who are good at solving problems are called this. (*resourceful*)

free	fuel	rule	cure	our
feel	refuel	ruler	sure	sour
us	ore	rules	four	scour
use	core	clue		source
useful	score	focus		resource
				resourceful

As students spell each word, write it on the board. Ask them to cross-check their spelling with yours and correct any errors. On the board or in a pocket chart, sort the words according to the following spelling patterns:

-ore	*-ure*	*-our*
ore	cure	sour
core	sure	four
score		our
		scour

After all the words have been spelled and sorted, have students read over the list, emphasizing the spelling pattern from the first vowel to the end of each word. In the case of multisyllabic words, the rimes are a bit different, so stress the rhymes of these words.

Tell students that these patterns can help them spell many other words. The Day 4 activity will start with these patterns.

Take an opportunity to talk about some of the following elements: prefixes/suffixes (*useful, resource, resourceful, refuel, ruler, rules*); spelling patterns that look alike but do not rhyme (*four, our*).

Day 4: Rhymer

Return to some of the patterns from the Day 3 lesson. With students, brainstorm a list of words using these rime patterns. This can be done in several different ways:

- The whole group brainstorms with you and makes a list.
- Assign the same or different patterns to partners or small groups. Have them create a list of words to share with the class.
- Make the small-group assignment competitive. Choose a pattern and let each group take turns adding a word to the list until only one group is able to add a word. You might want to let groups use a dictionary to verify their words.

Day 5: Word Smart

Distribute the Lesson 6 words and ask students to arrange them across the top of their desk with plenty of workspace below. Have students respond to your questions by picking up the correct word card(s) and holding it so you can see their answer. If there are more than two correct answers, tell students to show only two—one in each hand. Ask students, "Can you find the . . ."

- word that is the first part of the name of the first U.S. president?
- word that is part of *knowledge*?
- word that names the last part of the writing process before publishing?
- word that tells what electricity is?
- word that is what wind and water can produce?
- word that could describe a dictionary? an almanac?
- word hiding the word *now*? *new*? *ash*? *it*? *sour*? *for*? *no*?
- word that rhymes with *beehive*?
- word that fits in this sentence: "If you study, you will _____ the answers on the test."?
- word that is the opposite of *after*? *renewable*?
- word that has a prefix and a suffix?
- word that has 3 syllables?
- word that fits in this sentence: "Nonrenewable has _____ syllables."?
- word that is what water, wind, trees, and sun are?
- word with a long-*i* sound?
- word that starts with a vowel?
- word that is something you do to a face, a car, and your clothes?
- word that fits in this sentence: "Brush your teeth _____ you go to bed at night."?

✳ Homework ✳

After Day 5, words go home with students. They review the words and use them to complete the Parent-Child Word Work page (see page 128).

Day 1: Meet the Words

Have students pull apart the 8 word cards for this lesson and arrange the cards across the top of their desk. Then ask them to do the following:

- Hold up each card as you pronounce the word on it.
- Look at the word, read it aloud, and spell it with you.
- Return the word card to the top of their desk.

Say each word. Provide a simple definition as necessary and share some of its features as described below. You may want to have students use their fingers to cover certain letters to isolate phonic elements such as initial letters, blends, vowels, or hidden words, or point to certain letters as you discuss them. Clap the syllables in each word, and use it in a sentence that helps students understand the meaning of the word.

Some notable features of these words include the following:

* **where**: frequently-used word; often used as question word; /hw/ beginning sound as different from /w/; compare/contrast to the word *were*; hidden words: *he, here*

* **were**: frequently-used word; /w/ beginning sound; compare/contrast with *where*; use as verb; hidden word: *we*

* **when**: frequently-used word; often used as question word; /hw/ beginning; compare with beginning of *where*; hidden words: *he, hen*

* **or**: frequently-used word; word that shows choice; sometimes used with words in a series, and sometimes used as a coordinating conjunction; pattern used with *for, nor*

* **prefixes**: a prefix is a word part with its own meaning that comes at the beginning of a word; *pre-* means "before"; plural with *-es* (suffix); 3 syllables as plural; hidden words: *refix, fix, ref*

* **prewrite**: word used often in language arts; the first step in the process of writing that means "to plan what to say before composing ideas" (e.g., jot lists, brainstorm, outline, use graphic organizers); *pre-* is a prefix meaning "before"; *write* has a homophone—*right*, with a different spelling pattern and meaning; 2 syllables; hidden words: *rewrite* (with prefix *re-* meaning "again"—write again), *write, it*

* **distance**: word used often in math and in general use; means "the amount of space between two things/points" (*give examples*); can be measured in many ways—miles, feet, inches, centimeters, kilometers, light years, and so on; 2 syllables; hidden words: *is, tan, stance, an*

* **inches**: word used often in math; a measurement/distance (*show length of one inch*); brainstorm what types of things would be measured in inches; plural with *-es* (suffix); 2 syllables; hidden words: *in, inch, he*

Day 2: Word Whittle

Distribute the plastic bags containing this week's words or ask students to retrieve them. Have students place the words across the top of their workspace. After you read the first clue, they pull down all the words that fit it. For each subsequent clue in the set, students continue to whittle the words by returning those that don't fit to the top of their workspace. No new words can be added to the group after the first clue. Only one word will remain after the final clue in a set. Students return the word card to the top of their workspace before the next set of clues begins.

First Set:

1. a word that ends with e (*where, were, prewrite, distance*)
2. a word that has 2 *e*'s (*where, were, prewrite*)
3. a word that has a tall letter (*where, prewrite*)
4. a word that has 2 syllables (*prewrite*)

Second Set:

1. a word that has the little word *he* inside (*where, when, inches*)
2. a word that has a tall letter (*where, when, inches*)
3. a word that starts with a consonant (*where, when*)
4. a word related to time (*when*)

Third Set:

1. a word with 2 or more syllables (*prefixes, prewrite, distance, inches*)
2. a word that is plural (*prefixes, inches*)
3. a word that has 1 tall letter (*prefixes, inches*)
4. a word that relates to a short distance (*inches*)

Fourth Set:

1. a word that has 2 or more syllables and starts with a consonant (*prefixes, prewrite, distance*)
2. a word with a beginning word part that means "before" (*prefixes, prewrite*)
3. a word that has a letter that goes below the line (*prefixes, prewrite*)
4. a word that has 3 syllables (*prefixes*)

Stump the Class

Give pairs or small groups time to work together to find relationships among this week's words. Once they have found a category into which several of the words fit, they should write the

words in a circle on the Word Clusters sheet (see page 127) and the category underneath. Allow time for each pair or group to share one set of their words and ask the rest of the class to guess the category. Even though the other students may suggest a legitimate category, only the presenters' category is the correct answer. The goal is to stump the rest of the class with a unique category. (You might discover categories that you can add to the Day 5: Word Smart activity.)

Day 3: Word Builder

Have students separate the letters at the bottom of this week's word template. Ask them to spell words as you call them out. Have students construct words based on patterns in the words and call out words in increasingly difficult order as shown below. The final word should answer this clue: You use this with inches and distance. (*measurement*)

met	name	east	eat	menu
set	same	eastern	eaten	entree
team	tame	term	meat	amuse
teams	tamer	senate	ear	amusement
steam	must	ate	near	measure
seam	rust	mate	tear	measurement
seem		mates	smear	

As students spell each word, write it on the board. Ask them to cross-check their spelling with yours and correct any errors. On the board or in a pocket chart, sort the words according to the following spelling patterns:

-et	-eam	-ame	-ust	-ate	-ear
met	team	name	must	ate	ear
set	seam	same	rust	mate	near
		tame			tear
					smear

After all the words have been spelled and sorted, have students read over the list, emphasizing the spelling pattern from the first vowel to the end of each word. In the case of multisyllabic words, the rimes are a bit different, so stress the rhymes of these words.

Tell students that these patterns can help them spell many other words. The Day 4 activity will start with these patterns.

Take an opportunity to talk about some of the following elements: homophones (*seam/seem*), suffixes (*east/eastern, eat/eaten, tame/tamer*), suffixes for plurals (*-s*), verb tenses (*eat/eaten/ate*), meaning relationships (*menu/entree, tame/tamer, term/senate*).

Day 4: Rhymer

Return to some of the patterns from the Day 3 lesson. With students, brainstorm a list of words using these rime patterns. This can be done in several different ways:

- The whole group brainstorms with you and makes a list.
- Assign the same or different patterns to partners or small groups. Have them create a list of words to share with the class.
- Make the small-group assignment competitive. Choose a pattern and let each group take turns adding a word to the list until only one group is able to add a word. You might want to let groups use a dictionary to verify their words.

Day 5: Word Smart

Distribute the Lesson 7 words and ask students to arrange them across the top of their desk with plenty of workspace below. Have students respond to your questions by picking up the correct word card(s) and holding it so you can see their answer. If there are more than two correct answers, tell students to show only two—one in each hand. Ask students, "Can you find the . . ."

- word that starts with a /hw/ sound?
- word that asks a question?
- word that has a prefix that means "before"?
- word that is plural?
- word that starts with a vowel?
- word that has 2 syllables? 3 syllables?
- words that have all the same letters except for 1 letter?
- word that means "the space between two points"?
- word that means "something you do before you begin to compose your writing"?
- word that tells how many of these are in a foot?
- word hiding the little word *he*? *here*?
- word hiding the verb *is*?
- word that has the sound /ch/ inside?
- word hiding a hen?
- words that fit in this sentence: "The _____ between our ears is only about 6 _____."?

Day 1: Meet the Words

Have students pull apart the 8 word cards for this lesson and arrange the cards across the top of their desk. Then ask them to do the following:

- Hold up each card as you pronounce the word on it.
- Look at the word, read it aloud, and spell it with you.
- Return the word card to the top of their desk.

Say each word. Provide a simple definition as necessary and share some of its features as described below. You may want to have students use their fingers to cover certain letters to isolate phonic elements such as initial letters, blends, vowels, or hidden words, or point to certain letters as you discuss them. Clap the syllables in each word, and use it in a sentence that helps students understand the meaning of the word.

Some notable features of these words include the following:

* **then**: /th/ beginning sound; similarity to *than*; *-en* and *-in* often sound alike; helps in our reading/writing to show sequence, such as "Fold your paper in half, and then write your name on it."; hidden words: *he, hen*

* **could**: *c* makes the /k/ sound; /oŏ / sound; silent *l*; same spelling patterns for *would* and *should*; verb

* **ask**: short-*a* sound; whole word is a spelling pattern for words like *task, mask, bask*; helps make the *sk* blended sound

* **every**: short-*e* sound /e/; 2 syllables; *y* makes long-*e* sound; means "each one," as in "Every student will attend the program."; hidden word: *very*

* **draft**: *dr-* blend at beginning; short-*a* sound; enunciate the sound /ft/; multiple-meaning word: "stage of writing process after prewriting where writer gets ideas down on paper," or "the process of picking someone to do something they haven't volunteered to do"; hidden word: *raft*

* **singular**: starts with a snake sound; 3 syllables; means "one," as in "The word *boy* is singular and *boys* is plural. *Mouse* is singular and *mice* is plural."; *-ar* is *r*-controlled and says the letter name of *r*; hidden words: *sin, sing, in*

* **yard**: /y/ to start; *-ar* is *r*-controlled and says the letter name *r*; /d/ ending sound; multiple-meaning word: "measurement that is 3 feet or 36 inches" (*show example*), or "the space around someone's home," as in "Let's go out in the yard and play."

* **foot**: /f/ beginning sound; /oŏ/ sound; /t/ ending; multiple-meaning word: "measurement of 12 inches" (*show examples*), or "the appendage at the end of our leg that we walk on"

Day 2: Word Whittle

Distribute the plastic bags containing this week's words or ask students to retrieve them. Have students place the words across the top of their workspace. After you read the first clue, they pull down all the words that fit it. For each subsequent clue in the set, students continue to whittle the words by returning those that don't fit to the top of their workspace. No new words can be added to the group after the first clue. Only one word will remain after the final clue in a set. Students return the word card to the top of their workspace before the next set of clues begins.

First Set:

1. a word that has at least 1 tall letter (*then, could, ask, draft, singular, yard, foot*)
2. a word that has at least 2 tall letters (*then, could, draft, foot*)
3. a word that ends with a /t/ sound (*draft, foot*)
4. a word that means "12 inches" (*foot*)

Second Set:

1. a word that starts with a consonant (*then, could, draft, singular, yard, foot*)
2. a word that ends with a consonant (*then, could, draft, singular, yard, foot*)
3. a word that has 2 vowels together (*could, foot*)
4. a word that rhymes with *should* (*could*)

Third Set:

1. a word that has 4 letters (*then, yard, foot*)
2. a word that has 3 consonants (*then, yard*)
3. a word that has 1 syllable (*then, yard*)
4. a transition word that we use to tell what comes next (*then*)

Fourth Set:

1. a word whose first letter appears near the end of the alphabet (*then, singular, yard*)
2. a word with an *a* (*singular, yard*)
3. a word with 1 tall letter (*singular, yard*)
4. a word that has 3 syllables (*singular*)

Stump the Class

Give pairs or small groups time to work together to find relationships among this week's words. Once they have found a category into which several of the words fit, they should write the words in a circle on the Word Clusters sheet (see page 127) and the category underneath. Allow time for each pair or group to share one set of their words and ask the rest of the class to guess the category. Even though the other students may suggest a legitimate category, only the presenters' category is the correct answer. The goal is to stump the rest of the class with a unique category. (You might discover categories that you can add to the Day 5: Word Smart activity.)

Day 3: Word Builder

Have students separate the letters at the bottom of this week's word template. Ask them to spell words as you call them out. Have students construct words based on patterns in the words and call out words in increasingly difficult order as shown below. The final word should answer this clue: People who use measurements such as inch, foot, and yard in their job. (*carpenters*)

nest	car	space	scrap	cent
pest	scar	pace	scrape	center
rest	star	race	scraper	carpet
can	step	racer	partner	carpenter
scan	pets	rent	parent	carpenters
scant		spent	scent	

As students spell each word, write it on the board. Ask them to cross-check their spelling with yours and correct any errors. On the board or in a pocket chart, sort the words according to the following spelling patterns:

-est	*-an*	*-ar*	*-ace*	*-ent*
nest	can	car	space	rent
pest	scan	scar	pace	spent
rest		star	race	scent
				cent

After all the words have been spelled and sorted, have students read over the list, emphasizing the spelling pattern from the first vowel to the end of each word. In the case of multisyllabic words, the rimes are a bit different, so stress the rhymes of these words.

Tell students that these patterns can help them spell many other words. The Day 4 activity will start with these patterns.

Take an opportunity to talk about some of the following elements: homophones (*cent/scent*), suffixes (*scrape/scraper*, *race/racer*), suffixes for plurals (*-s*), verb tenses, and the numerous consonant blends with *sc-, sp-, scr-*.

Day 4: Rhymer

Return to some of the patterns from the Day 3 lesson. With students, brainstorm a list of words using these rime patterns. This can be done in several different ways:

- The whole group brainstorms with you and makes a list.

- Assign the same or different patterns to partners or small groups. Have them create a list of words to share with the class.
- Make the small-group assignment competitive. Choose a pattern and let each group take turns adding a word to the list until only one group is able to add a word. You might want to let groups use a dictionary to verify their words.

Day 5: Word Smart

Distribute the Lesson 8 words and ask students to arrange them across the top of their desk with plenty of workspace below. Have students respond to your questions by picking up the correct word card(s) and holding it so you can see their answer. If there are more than two correct answers, tell students to show only two—one in each hand. Ask students, "Can you find the . . ."

- word that starts with a /th/ sound?
- word that expects to get an answer?
- word that means "one of something"?
- word that is used to tell distance?
- word that has 3 syllables?
- word hiding a hen?
- word hiding the word *sing*? *very*?
- word hiding the name of something you might float down a river on?
- word that when combined with *ball* is the name of a sport?
- word that is the name of a place or means "36 inches or 3 feet"?
- word that means "each"?
- word that means "part of the writing process that comes after the prewrite stage"?
- word that fits in this sentence: "_____ you help me find the office."?
- word that starts with the same blend as *drink*?
- word that ends with the same consonant cluster as the word *task*?
- word that is the singular form of *feet*?
- word that names the unit used to measure the length of an item?
- word that is hiding a pronoun used instead of a boy's name?

✳ Homework ✳

After Day 5, words go home with students. They review the words and use them to complete the Parent-Child Word Work page (see page 128).

Day 1: Meet the Words

Have students pull apart the 8 word cards for this lesson and arrange the cards across the top of their desk. Then ask them to do the following:

- Hold up each card as you pronounce the word on it.
- Look at the word, read it aloud, and spell it with you.
- Return the word card to the top of their desk.

Say each word. Provide a simple definition as necessary and share some of its features as described below. You may want to have students use their fingers to cover certain letters to isolate phonic elements such as initial letters, blends, vowels, or hidden words, or point to certain letters as you discuss them. Clap the syllables in each word, and use it in a sentence that helps students understand the meaning of the word.

Some notable features of these words include the following:

* **write**: frequently-used word; verb; means "to compose"—put thoughts on paper; silent e; /r/ sound like beginning of *wrinkle*; homophone of *right*; spelling pattern helps spell words like *kite, bite, site, dynamite*; hidden word: *it*

* **always**: frequently-used word; adverb; means "each and every time," as in "We always start the day by reading."; 2 syllables; hidden words: *way, ways* (remind students that the word *all* has 2 *l*'s)

* **made**: frequently-used word; verb; slight changes to word change its meaning: *make, maker, making*; long *a*; silent e; homophone is *maid*; spelling pattern helps write words like *fade, jade, wade*; hidden words: *mad, ad, ma*

* **gave**: frequently-used word; verb; long-*a* sound; slight changes to word change its meaning: *give, giver, given*; spelling pattern helps spell words like *cave, pave, rave*

* **plot**: *l*-blend at beginning: *pl*; multiple meaning: 1) (*noun*) outline of important events in a story; and 2) (*verb*) to plan something secretly; spelling pattern helps spell words like *cot, dot, got, hot, jot, lot, not, pot*; hidden word: *lot*

* **infer**: means "to use clues and what you know to make predictions" ("Janie is folding her dripping umbrella as she comes in the door, so I infer that it must be raining outside."); 2 syllables, hidden word: *in*

* **investigate**: starts the same way as *infer*; means "to study and analyze something"; 4 syllables; hidden words: *in, vest, invest, gate, ate*

* **scientist**: someone whose career is to study some area of science; *-ist* suffix means "a person who does something related to [the first part of the word]": "A dentist is a person whose career is to do dental work."; 3 syllables; hidden word: *is*

Day 2: Word Whittle

Distribute the plastic bags containing this week's words or ask students to retrieve them. Have students place the words across the top of their workspace. After you read the first clue, they pull down all the words that fit it. For each subsequent clue in the set, students continue to whittle the words by returning those that don't fit to the top of their workspace. No new words can be added to the group after the first clue. Only one word will remain after the final clue in a set. Students return the word card to the top of their workspace before the next set of clues begins.

First Set:
1. a word that has an *a* (*always, made, gave, investigate*)
2. a word that has more than 1 syllable (*always, investigate*)
3. a word that starts with a vowel (*always, investigate*)
4. a word that has 4 syllables (*investigate*)

Second Set:
1. a word that has a silent e at the end (*write, made, gave, investigate*)
2. a word that has a vowel/consonant/vowel pattern at the end (*write, made, gave, investigate*)
3. words that are alike except for 2 letters (*made, gave*)
4. a word that, if you changed the first letter to *gr*, would name something you earn in class (*made*)

Third Set:
1. a word that has 2 of the same letter (*always, investigate, scientist*)
2. a word that starts with a vowel (*always, investigate*)
3. a word that has letters above and below the line (*always, investigate*)
4. a word that means "each and every time" (*always*)

Fourth Set:
1. a word that has an *i* (*write, infer, investigate, scientist*)
2. a word that starts with an *i* (*infer, investigate*)
3. a word whose first sound names a letter of the alphabet (*infer, investigate*)
4. a word that names something a good scientist does (*investigate*)

Stump the Class

Give pairs or small groups time to work together to find relationships among this week's words. Once they have found a category into which several of the words fit, they should write the words in a circle on the Word Clusters sheet (see page 127) and the category underneath. Allow time for each pair or group to share one set of their words and ask the rest of the class to guess the category. Even though the other students may suggest a legitimate category, only the presenters' category is the correct answer. The goal is to stump the rest of the class with a unique category. (You might discover categories that you can add to the Day 5: Word Smart activity.)

Day 3: Word Builder

Have students separate the letters at the bottom of this week's word template. Ask them to spell words as you call them out. Have students construct words based on patterns in the words and call out words in increasingly difficult order as shown below. The final word should answer this clue: In many TV shows, this person solves the mystery. (*investigator*)

tar	gave	eat	visit
target	grave	seat	visitor
vote	grove	sit	invest
voting	stove	sitting	investigator
voter	strive		

As students spell each word, write it on the board. Ask them to cross-check their spelling with yours and correct any errors. On the board or in a pocket chart, sort the words according to the following spelling patterns:

-ave	-ove	-eat
gave	grove	eat
grave	stove	seat

After all the words have been spelled and sorted, have students read over the list, emphasizing the spelling pattern from the first vowel to the end of each word. In the case of multisyllabic words, the rimes are a bit different, so stress the rhymes of these words.

Tell students that these patterns can help them spell many other words. The Day 4 activity will start with these patterns.

Take an opportunity to talk about some of the following elements: prefixes/suffixes (*sitting, visitor, investigator, voting, voter*).

Day 4: Rhymer

Return to some of the patterns from the Day 3 lesson. With students, brainstorm a list of words using these rime patterns. This can be done in several different ways:

- The whole group brainstorms with you and makes a list.
- Assign the same or different patterns to partners or small groups. Have them create a list of words to share with the class.
- Make the small-group assignment competitive. Choose a pattern and let each group take turns adding a word to the list until only one group is able to add a word. You might want to let groups use a dictionary to verify their words.

Day 5: Word Smart

Distribute the Lesson 9 words and ask students to arrange them across the top of their desk with plenty of workspace below. Have students respond to your questions by picking up the correct word card(s) and holding it so you can see their answer. If there are more than two correct answers, tell students to show only two—one in each hand. Ask students, "Can you find the . . ."

- word with the most syllables?
- word that rhymes with *dynamite*?
- word that rhymes with *got*?
- word that is hiding a synonym for *angry*?
- word hiding a piece of land?
- word that involves making a guess?
- word hiding a smaller word that means "to put your money into a project that earns more money"?
- word that begins and ends with a vowel?
- word that is a homophone for a word that means "correct"?
- word that is a homophone for the name of a person who cleans homes and offices?
- word that means "each and every time"?
- word that names a career?
- word that starts with the same blend as the word *play*?
- word that starts with a word part that is the opposite of *out*?
- word that is the past tense of *give*?

Day 1: Meet the Words

Have students pull apart the 8 word cards for this lesson and arrange the cards across the top of their desk. Then ask them to do the following:

- Hold up each card as you pronounce the word on it.
- Look at the word, read it aloud, and spell it with you.
- Return the word card to the top of their desk.

Say each word. Provide a simple definition as necessary and share some of its features as described below. You may want to have students use their fingers to cover certain letters to isolate phonic elements such as initial letters, blends, vowels, or hidden words, or point to certain letters as you discuss them. Clap the syllables in each word, and use it in a sentence that helps students understand the meaning of the word.

Some notable features of these words include the following:

✳ **very**: frequently-used word; adverb that tells how much—*very beautiful, very smooth, very tall*; /v/ beginning sound; *y* at end makes long-*e* sound

✳ **buy**: frequently-used word; verb that means "to purchase"; unusual spelling since -*uy* makes long-*i* sound; homophone of *by* and *bye*

✳ **those**: frequently-used word; /th/ beginning; long-*o* sound; silent *e* at end; -*ose* spelling pattern helps spell words like *pose, nose, dose, hose, rose*; hidden word: *hose*

✳ **use**: frequently-used word; verb, as in "Let's use a map to find our way"; also used as a noun ("computer use has increased"); long-*u* sound at beginning; silent *e* at end; hidden word: *us*

✳ **suffixes**: used often in language arts; added to the end of a base word to slightly change its meaning, such as *shoe, shoes* (changes from singular to plural), *sell, seller* (changes the action into the person who performs the action); -*es* on end of the word is a suffix that changes it from singular to plural; double consonant (*ff*); 3 syllables; hidden words: *fix, fixes*

✳ **dimensions**: term used often in math and science; measurements of an object; depending on shape of object, dimensions might be measured in different ways, such as length, height, width, circumference, area, perimeter, and so on; 3 syllables; hidden words: *dim, men, on, ion*

✳ **perimeter**: term used often in math; measurement around the boundary of an object (*give example*); word part *peri* means "around"; word part *meter* comes from Latin *metron* which means "measure"; 4 syllables; hidden words: *rim, meter, met, per, me*

✳ **circle**: term used often in math; something round in shape in which measurement through center in any direction is the same; word part *circ* means "round," as in *circular, circulate, circumference*; 2 syllables

Day 2: Word Whittle

Distribute the plastic bags containing this week's words or ask students to retrieve them. Have students place the words across the top of their workspace. After you read the first clue, they pull down all the words that fit it. For each subsequent clue in the set, students continue to whittle the words by returning those that don't fit to the top of their workspace. No new words can be added to the group after the first clue. Only one word will remain after the final clue in a set. Students return the word card to the top of their workspace before the next set of clues begins.

First Set:

1. a word that starts with a consonant (*very, buy, those, suffixes, dimensions, perimeter, circle*)
2. a word that has more than 1 syllable (*very, suffixes, dimensions, perimeter, circle*)
3. a word that is plural (*suffixes, dimensions*)
4. a word that refers to word parts added to the end of base words (*suffixes*)

Second Set:

1. a word that has a vowel for its second letter (*very, buy, suffixes, dimensions, perimeter, circle*)
2. a word that has at least 1 *s* (*suffixes, dimensions*)
3. a word that has 3 syllables (*suffixes, dimensions*)
4. a word that is hiding the plural for *man* (*dimensions*)

Third Set:

1. a word that has 1 syllable (*buy, those, use*)
2. a word that ends with an /s/ sound (*those, use*)
3. a word that has 2 vowels (*those, use*)
4. a word that can be a verb (*use*)

Fourth Set:

1. a word that has an *s* or makes an /s/ sound (*those, use, suffixes, dimensions, circle*)
2. a word that has a long vowel sound (*those, use*)
3. a word that has a vowel-consonant-vowel pattern (*those, use*)
4. a word that starts the same way as the word *them* (*those*)

Stump the Class

Give pairs or small groups time to work together to find relationships among this week's words. Once they have found a

category into which several of the words fit, they should write the words in a circle on the Word Clusters sheet (see page 127) and the category underneath. Allow time for each pair or group to share one set of their words and ask the rest of the class to guess the category. Even though the other students may suggest a legitimate category, only the presenters' category is the correct answer. The goal is to stump the rest of the class with a unique category. (You might discover categories that you can add to the Day 5: Word Smart activity.)

Day 3: Word Builder

Have students separate the letters at the bottom of this week's word template. Ask them to spell words as you call them out. Have students construct words based on patterns in the words and call out words in increasingly difficult order as shown below. The final word should answer this clue: These include length and width. (*dimensions*)

no	dine	some	miss	dimension
nose	nine	men	missed	dimensions
dose	mine	end	side	
does	dime	send	snide	
	dimes	mend	denim	
	dome	mind		

As students spell each word with their letters, write the word on the board, placing it with other words that have the same spelling pattern:

-ose	-ine	-end	-ide
nose	dine	send	side
dose	nine	mend	snide
	mine		

After all the words have been spelled and sorted, have students read over the list, emphasizing the spelling pattern from the first vowel to the end of each word. In the case of multisyllabic words, the rimes are a bit different, so stress the rhymes of these words.

Tell students that these patterns can help them spell many other words. The Day 4 activity will start with these patterns.

Take an opportunity to talk about some of the following elements: not all spelling patterns that are alike have the same sound patterns (*dome, some*); plurals (*dimensions, dimes*); verb tense (*miss, missed*).

Day 4: Rhymer

Return to some of the patterns from the Day 3 lesson. With students, brainstorm a list of words using these rime patterns. This can be done in several different ways:

- The whole group brainstorms with you and makes a list.

- Assign the same or different patterns to partners or small groups. Have them create a list of words to share with the class.

- Make the small-group assignment competitive. Choose a pattern and let each group take turns adding a word to the list until only one group is able to add a word. You might want to let groups use a dictionary to verify their words.

Day 5: Word Smart

Distribute the Lesson 10 words and ask students to arrange them across the top of their desk with plenty of workspace below. Have students respond to your questions by picking up the correct word card(s) and holding it so you can see their answer. If there are more than two correct answers, tell students to show only two—one in each hand. Ask students, "Can you find the . . ."

- word with the least number of letters?
- word that is the longest on the list?
- word that rhymes with *nose*? *my*?
- word hiding the word *rim*? *fix*?
- word hiding the plural for *man*? *us*?
- word with 4 syllables? 3 syllables?
- word that fits in the sentence: "His good grades made his parents _____ proud."?
- word that starts with the same letters as the word *think*?
- word that ends with the same letters as the word *bicycle*?
- word hiding a pronoun? (*use* and all words with *i*: stress that pronoun *I* is always capitalized)
- word with no angles or sharp edges?
- word that refers to word endings?
- word that ends with a long-*i* sound? a long-*e* sound?
- word with a silent-*e* ending?
- word that is a homophone for the word said when you are leaving?
- word that has the same word part as *circular*?
- word hiding a little word that names something used to water a garden?
- word that starts the same as the word *suffer*?

✳ Homework ✳

After Day 5, words go home with students. They review the words and use them to complete the Parent-Child Word Work page (see page 128).

Day 1: Meet the Words

Have students pull apart the 8 word cards for this lesson and arrange the cards across the top of their desk. Then ask them to do the following:

- Hold up each card as you pronounce the word on it.
- Look at the word, read it aloud, and spell it with you.
- Return the word card to the top of their desk.

Say each word. Provide a simple definition as necessary and share some of its features as described below. You may want to have students use their fingers to cover certain letters to isolate phonic elements such as initial letters, blends, vowels, or hidden words, or point to certain letters as you discuss them. Clap the syllables in each word, and use it in a sentence that helps students understand the meaning of the word.

Some notable features of these words include the following:

- ✳ **fast**: frequently-used word; multiple meanings: "quick" or "to decline food"; *-ast* pattern will help spell words like *cast, last, mast, past*; /st/ blend; hidden word: *as*
- ✳ **pull**: frequently-used word; *-ull* pattern will help spell other words; double consonants
- ✳ **both**: frequently-used word; long-*o* sound; /th/ ending
- ✳ **duty**: word used often in social studies and character ed; means "something that one is expected or required to do because it is morally or legally right"; ask, "What are our duties as citizens? What are our duties as students?"; final *y* makes long-*e* sound; 2 syllables
- ✳ **volunteer**: word used often in social studies and character ed; as noun means "a person who offers his services without pay"; as verb means "to offer services without pay"; ask, "What could a volunteer your age do to help your community?" "What could you volunteer to do at home that would help?"; double *e*'s make long-*e* sound; 3 syllables; hidden word: *tee* (as in *golf tee*)
- ✳ **contribution**: word used often in social studies and character ed; means "something given or shared to help"; synonyms: *gift, donation*; ask, "What contribution could our class make to help our community?"; word part *con* means "together" and *tribute* comes from Latin *tribuere* which means "to pay"; 4 syllables; suffix *-tion* changes *contribute* (*verb*) to *contribution* (*noun*); hidden words: *rib, but, con*
- ✳ **privilege**: word used often in social studies and character ed; multiple meanings: 1) "a special right given to some people beyond others" or 2) "a right shared by people living under a constitution, such as the privilege of freedom of

speech given to all U.S. citizens"; 3 syllables; silent-*e* ending; hidden word: *leg*
- ✳ **government**: word used often in social studies; means "the system by which a city, county, state, or nation is ruled"; *-ment* is suffix added to *govern*, changing it from verb to noun; 3 syllables; hidden words: *over, men, go, gov* (abbreviation for *governor*)

Day 2: Word Whittle

Distribute the plastic bags containing this week's words or ask students to retrieve them. Have students place the words across the top of their workspace. After you read the first clue, they pull down all the words that fit it. For each subsequent clue in the set, students continue to whittle the words by returning those that don't fit to the top of their workspace. No new words can be added to the group after the first clue. Only one word will remain after the final clue in a set. Students return the word card to the top of their workspace before the next set of clues begins.

First Set:

1. a word that starts with a letter that comes before *m* in the alphabet (*fast, both, duty, contribution, government*)
2. a word that has more than 1 syllable (*duty, contribution, government*)
3. a word that has a *t* (*duty, government, contribution*)
4. a word that means "something a person is expected or required to do" (*duty*)

Second Set:

1. a word that has more than 2 syllables (*volunteer, privilege, government, contribution*)
2. a word that has more than 1 tall letter (*volunteer, contribution*)
3. a word that has an *r* (*volunteer, contribution*)
4. a word that has 4 syllables (*contribution*)

Third Set:

1. a word whose last 2 letters are a vowel and a consonant (*volunteer, privilege, contribution, duty* [if *y* is considered vowel])
2. a word that has 3 syllables (*volunteer, privilege*)
3. a word that has 2 *e*'s (*volunteer, privilege*)
4. a word that could name a person (*volunteer*)

Fourth Set:

1. a word that has 1 syllable (*fast, pull, both*)
2. a word that has 2 tall letters (*fast, pull, both*)
3. a word that ends with 2 consonants (*fast, pull, both*)
4. a word that ends with the same letters as the word *that* begins with (*both*)

Stump the Class

Give pairs or small groups time to work together to find relationships among this week's words. Once they have found a category into which several of the words fit, they should write the words in a circle on the Word Clusters sheet (see page 127) and the category underneath. Allow time for each pair or group to share one set of their words and ask the rest of the class to guess the category. Even though the other students may suggest a legitimate category, only the presenters' category is the correct answer. The goal is to stump the rest of the class with a unique category. (You might discover categories that you can add to the Day 5: Word Smart activity.)

Day 3: Word Builder

Have students separate the letters at the bottom of this week's word template. Ask them to spell words as you call them out. Have students construct words based on patterns in the words and call out words in increasingly difficult order as shown below. The final word should answer this clue: The United States has this type of government. (*democracy*)

car	come	cry	care
race	comedy	core	dare
day	cream	yam	mare
cay	creamy	ram	mercy
may	dream	cram	demo
decay	came		democracy

As students spell each word, write it on the board. Ask them to cross-check their spelling with yours and correct any errors. On the board or in a pocket chart, sort the words according to the following spelling patterns:

-am	-are	-ay
yam	care	day
ram	dare	cay
cram	mare	may
		decay

After all the words have been spelled and sorted, have students read over the list, emphasizing the spelling pattern from the first vowel to the end of each word. In the case of multisyllabic words, the rimes are a bit different, so stress the rhymes of these words.

Tell students that these patterns can help them spell many other words. The Day 4 activity will start with these patterns.

Take the opportunity to repeat that the United States is a democracy because its citizens get to elect officials, such as the president, senators, governors, mayors, and so on.

Day 4: Rhymer

Return to some of the patterns from the Day 3 lesson. With students, brainstorm a list of words using these rime patterns. This can be done in several different ways:

- The whole group brainstorms with you and makes a list.
- Assign the same or different patterns to partners or small groups. Have them create a list of words to share with the class.
- Make the small-group assignment competitive. Choose a pattern and let each group take turns adding a word to the list until only one group is able to add a word. You might want to let groups use a dictionary to verify their words.

Day 5: Word Smart

Distribute the Lesson 11 words and ask students to arrange them across the top of their desk with plenty of workspace below. Have students respond to your questions by picking up the correct word card(s) and holding it so you can see their answer. If there are more than two correct answers, tell students to show only two—one in each hand. Ask students, "Can you find the . . ."

- word that is the longest in this lesson?
- word that rhymes with *bull*? *beauty*?
- word hiding the name of a body part?
- word hiding the antonym for *stop*?
- word with a prefix that means "together"?
- word that means the opposite of *slow*? *push*?
- word that means "not just one or the other"?
- word that ends with the same suffix as *education*?
- word that fits in this sentence: "I will _____ to keep our school clean by picking up paper around the building."?
- word with 3 syllables? 4 syllables?
- word that without its suffix means "to rule"?
- word that fits in this sentence: "Because of his good grades, he will have the _____ of sitting on the stage with the principal."?
- word that is often written on a door?
- word that is hiding the word that is the opposite of *under*?
- word hiding abbreviation for the person who is in charge of state government?
- word that fits in this sentence: "My _____ to the party will be to bake cupcakes."?

❋ Homework ❋

After Day 5, words go home with students. They review the words and use them to complete the Parent-Child Word Work page (see page 128).

Day 1: Meet the Words

Have students pull apart the 8 word cards for this lesson and arrange the cards across the top of their desk. Then ask them to do the following:

- Hold up each card as you pronounce the word on it.
- Look at the word, read it aloud, and spell it with you.
- Return the word card to the top of their desk.

Say each word. Provide a simple definition as necessary and share some of its features as described below. You may want to have students use their fingers to cover certain letters to isolate phonic elements such as initial letters, blends, vowels, or hidden words, or point to certain letters as you discuss them. Clap the syllables in each word, and use it in a sentence that helps students understand the meaning of the word.

Some notable features of these words include the following:

* **sit**: frequently-used word; *-it* spelling pattern will help with many words, such as *bit, pit, lit, split, transmit*; hidden word: *it*

* **which**: frequently-used word; often starts a question; /hw/ beginning; short *i* sound; /ch/ blend

* **read**: frequently-used word; heteronym (same meaning and spelling but is pronounced differently according to its use: "Please read me a story." (*ea* makes long-*e* sound) "He read a story to me last night." (past tense); hidden word: *ad*

* **glossary**: academic vocabulary for "a text feature of a dictionary, usually at the back of a book, that gives definitions and pronunciation guides for key words"; 3 syllables; double consonant; hidden words: *gloss, loss*

* **evaporation**: multiple meanings: 1) "to disappear" or 2) science word that means "the loss of liquid through vaporization" (steam); 5 syllables; suffix *-tion* added to base word *evaporate*; hidden words: *vapor, ration, ratio*

* **barometer**: science term for an instrument that measures atmospheric pressure, usually to determine weather changes; derived from Greek words: *baros* (weight) and *metre* (measure); 4 syllables; hidden words: *bar, me, met, meter, Rome* (with capital letter)

* **atmosphere**: multiple meanings: 1) science word for the air surrounding Earth or 2) the mood or environment, such as, "The atmosphere was very tense after the children had quarreled."; *ph* makes an /f/ sound; 3 syllables; hidden words: *at, sphere, here, he, her*

* **cycle**: in science means "a complete round or series of occurrences that repeat," such as a water cycle or life cycle; the word is related in meaning to circle and wheel (*bicycle* =

two wheels); each *c* has a different sound, /s/ and /k/; silent *e*; 2 syllables

Day 2: Word Whittle

Distribute the plastic bags containing this week's words or ask students to retrieve them. Have students place the words across the top of their workspace. After you read the first clue, they pull down all the words that fit it. For each subsequent clue in the set, students continue to whittle the words by returning those that don't fit to the top of their workspace. No new words can be added to the group after the first clue. Only one word will remain after the final clue in a set. Students return the word card to the top of their workspace before the next set of clues begins.

First Set:

1. a word that has 1 syllable (*sit, which, read*)
2. a word that has at least 1 tall letter (*sit, which, read*)
3. a word that has an *i* (*sit, which*)
4. a word that starts with the same sound as *where* (*which*)

Second Set:

1. a word that has more than 2 syllables (*glossary, evaporation, barometer, atmosphere*)
2. a word that has an *o* (*glossary, evaporation, barometer, atmosphere*)
3. a word that relates to air (*evaporation, barometer, atmosphere*)
4. a word that is an instrument that measures air pressure (*barometer*)

Third Set:

1. a word that starts with one of the first 5 letters of the alphabet (*evaporation, barometer, atmosphere, cycle*)
2. a word that ends with a vowel (*atmosphere, cycle*)
3. a word that has 1 letter below the line (*atmosphere, cycle*)
4. a word that makes an /f/ sound but has no *f* (*atmosphere*)

Fourth Set:

1. a word that has more than 1 syllable (*glossary, evaporation, barometer, atmosphere, cycle*)
2. a word that has more than 2 syllables (*glossary, evaporation, barometer, atmosphere*)
3. a word that has more than 3 syllables (*evaporation, barometer*)
4. a word that has more than 4 syllables (*evaporation*)

Stump the Class

Give pairs or small groups time to work together to find relationships among this week's words. Once they have found a category into which several of the words fit, they should write the

words in a circle on the Word Clusters sheet (see page 127) and the category underneath. Allow time for each pair or group to share one set of their words and ask the rest of the class to guess the category. Even though the other students may suggest a legitimate category, only the presenters' category is the correct answer. The goal is to stump the rest of the class with a unique category. (You might discover categories that you can add to the Day 5: Word Smart activity.)

Day 3: Word Builder

Have students separate the letters at the bottom of this week's word template. Ask them to spell words as you call them out. Have students construct words based on patterns in the words and call out words in increasingly difficult order as shown below. The final word should answer this clue: Astronauts go through this to reach outer space. (*atmosphere*)

map	shape	post	seam
tap	reshape	poster	team
pat	heat	hear	steam
pot	reheat	smear	storm
hot	preheat	shear	earth
shot	repeat	share	atmosphere

As students spell each word, write it on the board. Ask them to cross-check their spelling with yours and correct any errors. On the board or in a pocket chart, sort the words according to the following spelling patterns:

-ap	-ot	-eat	-ear	-eam
map	pot	heat	hear	seam
tap	hot	reheat	smear	team
	shot	preheat	shear	steam
		repeat		

After all the words have been spelled and sorted, have students read over the list, emphasizing the spelling pattern from the first vowel to the end of each word. In the case of multisyllabic words, the rimes are a bit different, so stress the rhymes of these words.

Tell students that these patterns can help them spell many other words. The Day 4 activity will start with these patterns.

Take an opportunity to talk about some of the following elements: prefix *re-* means "again," as in *reheat, repeat, reshape*; prefix *pre-* means "before," as in *preheat*; and relationship among *steam, atmosphere,* and *Earth*.

Day 4: Rhymer

Return to some of the patterns from the Day 3 lesson. With students, brainstorm a list of words using these rime patterns. This can be done in several different ways:

- The whole group brainstorms with you and makes a list.
- Assign the same or different patterns to partners or small groups. Have them create a list of words to share with the class.
- Make the small-group assignment competitive. Choose a pattern and let each group take turns adding a word to the list until only one group is able to add a word. You might want to let groups use a dictionary to verify their words.

Day 5: Word Smart

Distribute the Lesson 12 words and ask students to arrange them across the top of their desk with plenty of workspace below. Have students respond to your questions by picking up the correct word card(s) and holding it so you can see their answer. If there are more than two correct answers, tell students to show only two—one in each hand. Ask students, "Can you find the . . ."

- word that is the longest in this lesson? the shortest?
- word that may not be pronounced correctly unless you know how it's being used?
- word that has 5 syllables? 4 syllables? 3 syllables? 2 syllables?
- word that is a scientific instrument?
- word that is hiding a word that means "a shiny surface"?
- word that rhymes with *submit*? *bleed*? *bled*?
- word that means "something in a series that repeats itself"?
- word for the air that surrounds us?
- word that hides a word that tells what happens when a team scores fewer points than the competing team?
- word that fits in this sentence: "___ team are you pulling for."?
- word that sometimes has *bi-* or *tri-* before it?
- words that have pronouns in them?
- word in which the same letter makes an /s/ sound and a /k/ sound?
- word that is a text feature that helps you understand the meanings of important words?

✳ Homework ✳

After Day 5, words go home with students. They review the words and use them to complete the Parent-Child Word Work page (see page 128).

Day 1: Meet the Words

Have students pull apart the 8 word cards for this lesson and arrange the cards across the top of their desk. Then ask them to do the following:

- Hold up each card as you pronounce the word on it.
- Look at the word, read it aloud, and spell it with you.
- Return the word card to the top of their desk.

Say each word. Provide a simple definition as necessary and share some of its features as described below. You may want to have students use their fingers to cover certain letters to isolate phonic elements such as initial letters, blends, vowels, or hidden words, or point to certain letters as you discuss them. Clap the syllables in each word, and use it in a sentence that helps students understand the meaning of the word.

Some notable features of these words include the following:

✳ **why**: frequently-used word; academic word; /hw/ beginning; *y* makes long-*i* sound; *-y* pattern helps spell words such as *by, my, fry, cry*; often used at beginning of interrogative sentence

✳ **found**: frequently-used word; *-ound* pattern helps spell words such as *sound, mound, ground, hound*

✳ **because**: frequently-used word; signals cause-effect relationship; compound word; 2 syllables; hidden words: *be, cause, use, us*

✳ **economy**: word used often in social studies; long *e* at beginning; long-*e* sound at end; refers to the management of money; 4 syllables; hidden words: *no, my*

✳ **distribution**: word used often in social studies; prefix: *dis-* (from Latin word meaning "apart or away"); suffix *-tion* shows it is a noun; refers to how something such as a product is divided and given out; class example of distribution might be how pencils and paper are distributed to students; related to economy, how products are distributed to different stores; 4 syllables; hidden words: *rib, is, but, ion*

✳ **export**: word used often in social studies; word parts are important—prefix *ex-* = *out*, and base word *port* = *carry*, *export* = *carry out* (goods that are carried out of the country or region); related to word *transport* with word parts: *trans* = *across*, *port* = *carry*, *transport* = *carry across*; 2 syllables; hidden words: *port, or*

✳ **import**: word used often in social studies; word parts are important—prefix *im-* = *in*, and base word *port* = *carry*, *import* = *carry in*, or goods that are brought into the country or region; relate to *transport* and *export*; 2 syllables; hidden words: *port, or*

✳ **abbreviation**: word used often in language arts but also general usage; remember the 2 *b*'s; first *i* makes long-*e* sound like the sound of *e* before it; *abbreviate* refers to shortening something; suffix *-tion* makes it a noun; often used to refer to shortened form of a word—examples: states (*SC, IN, CA*), titles for people (*Mr., Mrs., Dr., Rev.*); 5 syllables; hidden words: *via, at, ion, on*

Day 2: Word Whittle

Distribute the plastic bags containing this week's words or ask students to retrieve them. Have students place the words across the top of their workspace. After you read the first clue, they pull down all the words that fit it. For each subsequent clue in the set, students continue to whittle the words by returning those that don't fit to the top of their workspace. No new words can be added to the group after the first clue. Only one word will remain after the final clue in a set. Students return the word card to the top of their workspace before the next set of clues begins.

First Set:

1. a word that starts with a consonant (*why, found, because, distribution*)
2. a word that has at least 1 tall letter (*why, found, because, distribution*)
3. a word that has at least 2 tall letters (*found, distribution*)
4. a word that ends in 2 consonants (*found*)

Second Set:

1. a word that relates to buying and selling products (*economy, distribution, export, import*)
2. a word that has more than 2 syllables (*economy, distribution*)
3. a word that has more than 3 syllables (*economy, distribution*)
4. a word that refers to dividing products and giving them out (*distribution*)

Third Set:

1. a word that has 2 of the same letters (*because, economy, distribution, abbreviation*)
2. a word that starts with a vowel (*economy, abbreviation*)
3. a word that has more than 3 syllables (*economy, abbreviation*)
4. *Mr., Mrs.,* and *Dr.* are examples of this (*abbreviation*)

Fourth Set:

1. a word that starts with a vowel (*economy, export, import, abbreviation*)
2. a word that has a prefix that means "in" or "out" (*export, import*)
3. a word that has 2 syllables (*export, import*)
4. a word that means to send out a product (*export*)

Stump the Class

Give pairs or small groups time to work together to find relationships among this week's words. Once they have found a category into which several of the words fit, they should write the words in a circle on the Word Clusters sheet (see page 127) and the category underneath. Allow time for each pair or group to share one set of their words and ask the rest of the class to guess the category. Even though the other students may suggest a legitimate category, only the presenters' category is the correct answer. The goal is to stump the rest of the class with a unique category. (You might discover categories that you can add to the Day 5: Word Smart activity.)

Day 3: Word Builder

Have students separate the letters at the bottom of this week's word template. Ask them to spell words as you call them out. Have students construct words based on patterns in the words and call out words in increasingly difficult order as shown below. The final word should answer this clue: These turn Texas into TX and Missouri into MO. (*abbreviations*)

above	rain	rave	vine	oven
over	brain	brave	orbit	vision
on	stain	sir	sit	revision
in	strain	stir	visit	abbreviations
invite			visitor	

As students spell each word, write it on the board. Ask them to cross-check their spelling with yours and correct any errors. On the board or in a pocket chart, sort the words according to the following spelling patterns:

-ain	-ave	-it
rain	rave	sit
brain	brave	visit
stain		
strain		

After all the words have been spelled and sorted, have students read over the list, emphasizing the spelling pattern from the first vowel to the end of each word. In the case of multisyllabic words, the rimes are a bit different, so stress the rhymes of these words.

Tell students that these patterns can help them spell many other words. The Day 4 activity will start with these patterns.

Take an opportunity to talk about some of the following elements: prepositions (*over, on, in*); prefix *re-*; suffixes *-or* and *-tion*.

Day 4: Rhymer

Return to some of the patterns from the Day 3 lesson. With students, brainstorm a list of words using these rime patterns. This can be done in several different ways:

- The whole group brainstorms with you and makes a list.
- Assign the same or different patterns to partners or small groups. Have them create a list of words to share with the class.
- Make the small-group assignment competitive. Choose a pattern and let each group take turns adding a word to the list until only one group is able to add a word. You might want to let groups use a dictionary to verify their words.

Day 5: Word Smart

Distribute the Lesson 13 words and ask students to arrange them across the top of their desk with plenty of workspace below. Have students respond to your questions by picking up the correct word card(s) and holding it so you can see their answer. If there are more than two correct answers, tell students to show only two—one in each hand. Ask students, "Can you find the . . ."

- word that is the longest in this lesson? the shortest?
- word with a suffix that makes it a noun?
- word with a prefix that means "out"? "in"?
- word with a word part that means "carry"?
- word that starts many questions?
- word that is a compound?
- word that has 5 syllables? 1 syllable?
- word hiding the opposite of *yes*?
- word hiding a word part that means "three"?
- word hiding a bone in your body?
- word that fits in this sentence: "When the _____ is good, we eat out more often."?
- word that rhymes with *ground*?
- word that starts with the same prefix as *expense*?
- word that ends with the same suffix as *punctuation*?
- word that has a double consonant?
- word that ends with a long-*i* sound?
- word that refers to dividing and sending something out?

Day 1: Meet the Words

Have students pull apart the 8 word cards for this lesson and arrange the cards across the top of their desk. Then ask them to do the following:

- Hold up each card as you pronounce the word on it.
- Look at the word, read it aloud, and spell it with you.
- Return the word card to the top of their desk.

Say each word. Provide a simple definition as necessary and share some of its features as described below. You may want to have students use their fingers to cover certain letters to isolate phonic elements such as initial letters, blends, vowels, or hidden words, or point to certain letters as you discuss them. Clap the syllables in each word, and use it in a sentence that helps students understand the meaning of the word.

Some notable features of these words include the following:

✳ **best**: frequently-used word; -est pattern helps spell many other words such as *test, nest, west, arrest, vest, digest*; -st consonant blend; hidden word: *be*

✳ **upon**: frequently-used word; used to introduce fairy tales: "Once upon a time . . ."; preposition like *over, under, beneath*; 2 syllables; hidden words: *up, on*

✳ **these**: frequently-used word; /th/ at beginning; long-e sound; pronoun ("I want a pound of these.") or adjective ("I want several of these flowers."); hidden words: *the, he*

✳ **predict**: academic vocabulary; prefix *pre-* means "before"; *predict* means "to guess what is going to happen, based on clues if they are available"; *prediction* is the guess; /ct/ blend at end; 2 syllables; hidden word: *red*

✳ **symmetry**: used most often in math; word part *sym* means "together"; word part *metr* comes from *meter*, which means "measure"; means "when a line can be drawn through a figure and the two parts are equal"; a figure that has symmetry is referred to as symmetrical; notice double consonant; 3 syllables; hidden words: *me, met, try*

✳ **congruent**: used most often in math; word part *con* means "with or together"; means "two shapes are identical in size"; relationship between *symmetry* and *congruent*: a shape that has symmetry has 2 congruent sides when divided by a line; can be used to refer to ideas or opinions that are the same; 3 syllables; hidden word: *on*

✳ **polygon**: used often in math; word part *poly* means "many"; word part *gon* comes from word *gonia* which means "angle"; means "a closed shape that has at least 3 sides and 3 angles"; 3 syllables; hidden word: *go*

✳ **intersecting**: used often in math; prefix *inter-* means "between"; word part *sect* comes from Latin *secare* meaning "cut"; in math, means "lines that have one or more points in common (or that cross each other)," such as, "The curved lines are intersecting three times."; common use refers to streets and highways that cross, such as "The store is located where Main Street and Conners Avenue intersect"; 4 syllables; -ing ending; hidden words: *intersect, in, sect*

Day 2: Word Whittle

Distribute the plastic bags containing this week's words or ask students to retrieve them. Have students place the words across the top of their workspace. After you read the first clue, they pull down all the words that fit it. For each subsequent clue in the set, students continue to whittle the words by returning those that don't fit to the top of their workspace. No new words can be added to the group after the first clue. Only one word will remain after the final clue in a set. Students return the word card to the top of their workspace before the next set of clues begins.

First Set:
1. a word that has 3 syllables (*symmetry, congruent, polygon*)
2. a word that has letters that go below the line (*symmetry, congruent, polygon*)
3. a word that has 1 tall letter (*symmetry, congruent, polygon*)
4. a word that has a word part that means "many" (*polygon*)

Second Set:
1. a word with a consonant as the first letter (*best, these, predict, symmetry, congruent, polygon*)
2. a word with a consonant as the second letter (*these, predict*)
3. a word with 1 or more syllables (*these, predict*)
4. a word with a prefix that means "before" (*predict*)

Third Set:
1. a word used often in math (*predict, symmetry, congruent, polygon, intersecting*)
2. a word that has 3 syllables (*symmetry, congruent, polygon*)
3. a word that has a *y* (*symmetry, polygon*)
4. a word that fits in this sentence: "A shape has _____ when both its halves are congruent." (*symmetry*)

Fourth Set:
1. a word that has a *t* (*best, these, predict, symmetry, congruent, intersecting*)
2. a word that has no more than 2 syllables (*best, these, predict*)
3. a word that has an *s* (*best, these*)
4. a word that can help you spell the word *invest* (*best*)

Stump the Class

Give pairs or small groups time to work together to find relationships among this week's words. Once they have found a category into which several of the words fit, they should write the words in a circle on the Word Clusters sheet (see page 127) and the category underneath. Allow time for each pair or group to share one set of their words and ask the rest of the class to guess the category. Even though the other students may suggest a legitimate category, only the presenters' category is the correct answer. The goal is to stump the rest of the class with a unique category. (You might discover categories that you can add to the Day 5: Word Smart activity.)

Day 3: Word Builder

Have students separate the letters at the bottom of this week's word template. Ask them to spell words as you call them out. Have students construct words based on patterns in the words and call out words in increasingly difficult order as shown below. The final word should answer this clue: This polygon has 3 sides. (*triangle*)

rain	lint	stare	rang	alert
gain	glint	glare	ring	angel
train	stag	large	sing	angle
	stage	larger	sling	triangle
	steal	ear	sting	
		gear		

As students spell each word, write it on the board. Ask them to cross-check their spelling with yours and correct any errors. On the board or in a pocket chart, sort the words according to the following spelling patterns:

-ain	-int	-are	-ear	-ing
rain	lint	stare	ear	ring
gain	glint	glare	gear	sing
train				sling
				sting

After all the words have been spelled and sorted, have students read over the list, emphasizing the spelling pattern from the first vowel to the end of each word. In the case of multisyllabic words, the rimes are a bit different, so stress the rhymes of these words.

Tell students that these patterns can help them spell many other words. The Day 4 activity will start with these patterns.

Take an opportunity to talk about some of the following elements: consonant blend (*st-*); verb tense (*ring, rang*); superlatives (*large, larger*).

Day 4: Rhymer

Return to some of the patterns from the Day 3 lesson. With students, brainstorm a list of words using these rime patterns. This can be done in several different ways:

- The whole group brainstorms with you and makes a list.
- Assign the same or different patterns to partners or small groups. Have them create a list of words to share with the class.
- Make the small-group assignment competitive. Choose a pattern and let each group take turns adding a word to the list until only one group is able to add a word. You might want to let groups use a dictionary to verify their words.

Day 5: Word Smart

Distribute the Lesson 14 words and ask students to arrange them across the top of their desk with plenty of workspace below. Have students respond to your questions by picking up the correct word card(s) and holding it so you can see their answer. If there are more than two correct answers, tell students to show only two—one in each hand. Ask students, "Can you find the . . ."

- word that has 4 syllables?
- word that has a word part that means "measure"?
- word that has a prefix that means "before"?
- word that is in the first line of many fairy tales?
- word that rhymes with *interest*? *please*?
- word hiding the word *met*? *red*? *up*?
- word with a prefix that means "between"?
- word that tells which ones?
- word that means "to make a guess about something that will happen"?
- word that describes 2 closed shapes that are identical?
- word that names a shape?
- word that refers to lines that cross each other?
- word that is the opposite of *worst*?
- word that is a compound word?
- word that comes from word parts that mean "many angles"?
- word that rhymes with *licked* but is spelled differently?
- word that means the two halves of a shape exactly match?
- word that rhymes with *breeze* but is not spelled with the same pattern?

❄ Homework ❄

After Day 5, words go home with students. They review the words and use them to complete the Parent-Child Word Work page (see page 128).

Day 1: Meet the Words

Have students pull apart the 8 word cards for this lesson and arrange the cards across the top of their desk. Then ask them to do the following:

- Hold up each card as you pronounce the word on it.
- Look at the word, read it aloud, and spell it with you.
- Return the word card to the top of their desk.

Say each word. Provide a simple definition as necessary and share some of its features as described below. You may want to have students use their fingers to cover certain letters to isolate phonic elements such as initial letters, blends, vowels, or hidden words, or point to certain letters as you discuss them. Clap the syllables in each word, and use it in a sentence that helps students understand the meaning of the word.

Some notable features of these words include the following:

✳ **sing**: frequently-used word; -ing spelling pattern helps spell many words; irregular tense changes: sing, sang, sung; hidden words: in, sin

✳ **wish**: frequently-used word; -ish spelling pattern helps spell many words; /sh/ blend; hidden word: is

✳ **many**: frequently-used word; same pattern as any; hidden words: man, any, ma

✳ **habitat**: word used often in science; means "the natural environment where a population or organism usually lives"; for example, rivers and oceans are the habitat for fish, deserts are the habitat for some reptiles, and cold, icy places are the habitat for penguins; 3 syllables; hidden words: habit, it, bit, at

✳ **offspring**: word used often in science; means "the children of a parent"; synonym for descendants; compound word whose component parts help explain its meaning; rhymes with this week's word, sing; 2 syllables; hidden words: off, spring, in, of, ring

✳ **parent**: frequently-used word and often used in science; means "a father or a mother or any organism that produces another"; 2 syllables; hidden words: rent, pa, are, pare

✳ **depend**: frequently-used word and often used in science; means "to rely on or trust" (I depend on my brother to drive me to the movies." "A baby must depend on its parents to survive."); 2 syllables; hidden words: end, pen

✳ **heredity**: word used often in science; means "the traits passed down from parents to offspring"–for example, eye and hair color, height, or a butterfly's size or markings; 4 syllables; hidden words: he, her, here, red, edit, it

Day 2: Word Whittle

Distribute the plastic bags containing this week's words or ask students to retrieve them. Have students place the words across the top of their workspace. After you read the first clue, they pull down all the words that fit it. For each subsequent clue in the set, students continue to whittle the words by returning those that don't fit to the top of their workspace. No new words can be added to the group after the first clue. Only one word will remain after the final clue in a set. Students return the word card to the top of their workspace before the next set of clues begins.

First Set:

1. a word that has 2 syllables (offspring, parent, depend)
2. a word that has 2 of the same letters (offspring, depend)
3. a word that has 2 tall letters (offspring, depend)
4. a word that is a compound (offspring)

Second Set:

1. a word that has 4 letters (sing, wish, many)
2. a word with a letter below the line (sing, many)
3. a word with 2 consonants (sing, many)
4. a word that hides a word for a grown-up boy (many)

Third Set:

1. a word that has an i (sing, wish, habitat, offspring, heredity)
2. a word that is used often in science (habitat, offspring, heredity)
3. a word that has more than 2 syllables (habitat, heredity)
4. a word that is hiding something that becomes regular or a routine (habitat)

Fourth Set:

1. a word that has more than 1 tall letter (habitat, offspring, depend, heredity)
2. a word that goes below the line (offspring, depend, heredity)
3. a word that has 2 pronouns inside (heredity)

Stump the Class

Give pairs or small groups time to work together to find relationships among this week's words. Once they have found a category into which several of the words fit, they should write the words in a circle on the Word Clusters sheet (see page 127) and the category underneath. Allow time for each pair or group to share one set of their words and ask the rest of the class to guess the category. Even though the other students may suggest a legitimate category, only the presenters' category is the correct answer. The goal is to stump the rest of the class with a unique category. (You might discover categories that you can add to the Day 5: Word Smart activity.)

Day 3: Word Builder

Have students separate the letters at the bottom of this week's word template. Ask them to spell words as you call them out. Have students construct words based on patterns in the words and call out words in increasingly difficult order as shown below. The final word should answer this clue: All the offspring of a set of parents create this. (*generation*)

go	tone	age	tore
toe	gone	rage	ignore
got	tiger	enrage	generation
not	anger	teen	
rot	agree	green	
gain	eat	orange	
regain	eaten		
	neat		

As students spell each word, write it on the board. Ask them to cross-check their spelling with yours and correct any errors. On the board or in a pocket chart, sort the words according to the following spelling patterns:

-ot	-ain	-one	-eat	-een	-ore	-age
got	gain	tone	eat	teen	tore	rage
not	regain	gone	neat	green	ignore	enrage
rot						

After all the words have been spelled and sorted, have students read over the list, emphasizing the spelling pattern from the first vowel to the end of each word. In the case of multisyllabic words, the rimes are a bit different, so stress the rhymes of these words.

Tell students that these patterns can help them spell many other words. The Day 4 activity will start with these patterns.

Take an opportunity to talk about some of the following elements: *go/toe* difference in pattern; verb tense (*eat, eaten*); colors (*green, orange*).

Day 4: Rhymer

Return to some of the patterns from the Day 3 lesson. With students, brainstorm a list of words using these rime patterns. This can be done in several different ways:

- The whole group brainstorms with you and makes a list.

- Assign the same or different patterns to partners or small groups. Have them create a list of words to share with the class.

- Make the small-group assignment competitive. Choose a pattern and let each group take turns adding a word to the list until only one group is able to add a word. You might want to let groups use a dictionary to verify their words.

Day 5: Word Smart

Distribute the Lesson 15 words and ask students to arrange them across the top of their desk with plenty of workspace below. Have students respond to your questions by picking up the correct word card(s) and holding it so you can see their answer. If there are more than two correct answers, tell students to show only two—one in each hand. Ask students, "Can you find the . . ."

- word that has 4 syllables?

- word that is a compound?

- word that is hiding something you pay if you don't own a home?

- word that is hiding a season?

- word that is hiding a color?

- word that names a kind of place?

- word that is a synonym for *children*?

- word that, if you replaced the first letter with a *d*, would be something you could eat out of?

- word that has 3 syllables?

- word that is hiding the partner for *ma*?

- words that fit in this sentence: "_____ inherit traits of their _____."?

- word that is hiding the opposite of *on*?

- word that is a synonym for *rely*?

- word that, if you changed the first letter, you could wear on your finger?

- word hiding the opposite of *beginning*?

- words that represent these two animals—cub and mother bear?

- word that fits in this sentence: "We _____ on each other for help in this classroom."?

- word hiding a father?

- word that is hiding something you do time and time again?

- words that rhyme with each other?

✲ Homework ✲

After Day 5, words go home with students. They review the words and use them to complete the Parent-Child Word Work page (see page 128).

Day 1: Meet the Words

Have students pull apart the 8 word cards for this lesson and arrange the cards across the top of their desk. Then ask them to do the following:

- Hold up each card as you pronounce the word on it.
- Look at the word, read it aloud, and spell it with you.
- Return the word card to the top of their desk.

Say each word. Provide a simple definition as necessary and share some of its features as described below. You may want to have students use their fingers to cover certain letters to isolate phonic elements such as initial letters, blends, vowels, or hidden words, or point to certain letters as you discuss them. Clap the syllables in each word, and use it in a sentence that helps students understand the meaning of the word.

Some notable features of these words include the following:

✳ **if**: frequently-used word; short-*i* sound; often signals a cause/ effect relationship

✳ **long**: frequently-used word; /ng/ blend; -*ong* helps spell other words such as *song, along, belong, lifelong, wrong, strong*; hidden words: *on, lo*

✳ **about**: frequently-used word; preposition like *on, over, under, beneath*; -*out* helps spell words such as *cookout, pout, out, scout*; 2 syllables; hidden words: *out, bout, a*

✳ **product**: word used in social studies; related to economics: "something made by labor that is made available for others by a company"; 2 syllables; hidden words: *rod, duct, pro, prod*

✳ **produce**: word used in social studies, related to economics; multiple-meaning word; heteronym: has same spelling but different meanings and different pronunciations: as noun with stress on first syllable—"agricultural goods such as fruits and vegetables," as in "We will buy lots of healthy produce at the farmers' market."; as verb with stress on second syllable—"to make, provide or manufacture," as in "We will produce a play this year in our class."; also used in science, as in "Producers are plants that make their own food."; 2 syllables; hidden words: *pro, rod, prod*

✳ **services**: word used in social studies, related to economics; means "something provided that is helpful to others," as in "Our soldiers provide valuable services to our country." Or, "Nurses, doctors, plumbers, and electricians provide services for all of us."; related to word *serve*; 3 syllables; hidden words: *vice, vices, ice, ices*

✳ **goods**: word used in social studies, related to economics; means "articles of trade, something produced," as in "The store buys and sells goods."; hidden words: *go, goo, good*

✳ **barter**: word used in social studies, related to economics; means "to trade," as in "He is able to barter some fresh eggs from his neighbor in exchange for firewood."; 2 syllables; hidden words: *bar, art*

Day 2: Word Whittle

Distribute the plastic bags containing this week's words or ask students to retrieve them. Have students place the words across the top of their workspace. After you read the first clue, they pull down all the words that fit it. For each subsequent clue in the set, students continue to whittle the words by returning those that don't fit to the top of their workspace. No new words can be added to the group after the first clue. Only one word will remain after the final clue in a set. Students return the word card to the top of their workspace before the next set of clues begins.

First Set:

1. a word that has 1 syllable (*if, long, goods*)
2. a word that has a *g* at the beginning or end (*long, goods*)
3. a word that has an *o* as its second letter (*long, goods*)
4. a word that could be cloth, furniture, pots and pans, or toys (*goods*)

Second Set:

1. a word with 2 syllables (*about, product, produce, barter*)
2. a word that has at least 1 tall letter (*about, product, produce, barter*)
3. a word that has the same beginning as *pronoun* (*product, produce*)
4. a word that means "to make or manufacture something" (*produce*)

Third Set:

1. a word that names a person, place, or thing—a noun (*product, produce, services, goods*)
2. a word that has at least 2 syllables (*product, produce, services*)
3. words that have all except 1 letter in common (*product, produce*)
4. a word with a silent letter at the end (*produce*)

Fourth Set:

1. a word that has an *o* (*long, about, product, produce, goods*)
2. a word that has at least 1 letter below the line (*long, product, produce, goods*)
3. a word that has 1 syllable (*long, goods*)
4. a word that rhymes with *strong* (*long*)

Stump the Class

Give pairs or small groups time to work together to find relationships among this week's words. Once they have found a category into which several of the words fit, they should write the words in a circle on the Word Clusters sheet (see page 127) and the category underneath. Allow time for each pair or group to share one set of their words and ask the rest of the class to guess the category. Even though the other students may suggest a legitimate category, only the presenters' category is the correct answer. The goal is to stump the rest of the class with a unique category. (You might discover categories that you can add to the Day 5: Word Smart activity.)

Day 3: Word Builder

Have students separate the letters at the bottom of this week's word template. Ask them to spell words as you call them out. Have students construct words based on patterns in the words and call out words in increasingly difficult order as shown below. The final word should answer this clue: Shoppers need to be smart about this! (*purchasing*)

cash	pacing	crush	push
cashing	racing	crushing	pushing
rash	caring	shaping	sharing
crashing	rush	scraping	panic
	rushing		spinach
			purchasing

As students spell each word, write it on the board. Ask them to cross-check their spelling with yours and correct any errors. On the board or in a pocket chart, sort the words according to the following spelling patterns:

-ash	-ush
cash	rush
rash	crush
	push

After all the words have been spelled and sorted, have students read over the list, emphasizing the spelling pattern from the first vowel to the end of each word. In the case of multisyllabic words, the rimes are a bit different, so stress the rhymes of these words.

Tell students that these patterns can help them spell many other words. The Day 4 activity will start with these patterns.

Take an opportunity to talk about some of the following elements: adding *-ing* to base words; removing the final *e* to add *-ing*.

Day 4: Rhymer

Return to some of the patterns from the Day 3 lesson. With students, brainstorm a list of words using these rime patterns. This can be done in several different ways:

- The whole group brainstorms with you and makes a list.
- Assign the same or different patterns to partners or small groups. Have them create a list of words to share with the class.
- Make the small-group assignment competitive. Choose a pattern and let each group take turns adding a word to the list until only one group is able to add a word. You might want to let groups use a dictionary to verify their words.

Day 5: Word Smart

Distribute the Lesson 16 words and ask students to arrange them across the top of their desk with plenty of workspace below. Have students respond to your questions by picking up the correct word card(s) and holding it so you can see their answer. If there are more than two correct answers, tell students to show only two—one in each hand. Ask students, "Can you find the . . ."

- word that rhymes with *stiff*? *strong*?
- word that has 3 syllables?
- word that is hiding something we might produce with a brush and paint?
- word that is hiding a long shelf that you might have in your kitchen?
- word that refers to something a person might buy?
- word hiding the opposite of *stop*?
- word that is a verb that means "to make or manufacture something"?
- word that starts with a vowel?
- word that rhymes with *blowout* and *scout*?
- word that means "something provided to help others"?
- word that fits in this sentence: "We will buy _____ at the grocery store today."?
- word that fits in this sentence: "Plumbers and carpenters provide _____."?
- word that is a synonym for *trade*?
- word that fits in this sentence: "I will buy a dog _____ I make enough money."?

✳ Homework ✳

After Day 5, words go home with students. They review the words and use them to complete the Parent-Child Word Work page (see page 128).

Day 1: Meet the Words

Have students pull apart the 8 word cards for this lesson and arrange the cards across the top of their desk. Then ask them to do the following:

- Hold up each card as you pronounce the word on it.
- Look at the word, read it aloud, and spell it with you.
- Return the word card to the top of their desk.

Say each word. Provide a simple definition as necessary and share some of its features as described below. You may want to have students use their fingers to cover certain letters to isolate phonic elements such as initial letters, blends, vowels, or hidden words, or point to certain letters as you discuss them. Clap the syllables in each word, and use it in a sentence that helps students understand the meaning of the word.

Some notable features of these words include the following:

✳ **got**: frequently-used word; -ot pattern used to spell many other words such as *slot, lot, cot, blot, bloodshot*; past tense of *get*; hidden word: *go*

✳ **six**: frequently-used word, especially in math; word pattern -ix used to spell other words such as *suffix, prefix, fix, mix*

✳ **never**: frequently-used word; hidden word: *ever*

✳ **sequential**: used often in content areas and language arts; refers to a natural order of events or numbers; good to recognize in reading as an organizational pattern and to use in writing to organize; adjective; base word is *sequence*; 3 syllables

✳ **fiction**: used often in language arts; narrative text that is not true—imaginative narrative; includes many different genres such as historical fiction, science fiction, mysteries, fables, fairy tales, legends, folktales; -tion makes "shun" sound; 2 syllables; hidden word: *on*

✳ **nonfiction**: used often in language arts; text that is factual/true; deals with facts and reality; includes different genres such as informational, biographies, autobiographies; *non-* means "not," as in "not fictional"; 3 syllables; hidden words: *no, on*

✳ **fable**: used most often in language arts; genre of fiction in which animals and lifelike objects teach a lesson; -able pattern used to spell other words such as *table, stable, able*; 2 syllables; hidden word: *fab* (slang), *able*

✳ **purpose**: academic vocabulary, used often in language arts, as in "author's purpose" or "reading for a purpose"; means "the goal, end, or intended result"; *o* is tricky because it sounds like /ə/, so make note of it; 2 syllables; hidden word: *pose*

Day 2: Word Whittle

Distribute the plastic bags containing this week's words or ask students to retrieve them. Have students place the words across the top of their workspace. After you read the first clue, they pull down all the words that fit it. For each subsequent clue in the set, students continue to whittle the words by returning those that don't fit to the top of their workspace. No new words can be added to the group after the first clue. Only one word will remain after the final clue in a set. Students return the word card to the top of their workspace before the next set of clues begins.

First Set:

1. a word that has 2 syllables (*never, fiction, fable, purpose*)
2. a word that has a letter that comes after *m* in the alphabet (*never, fiction, purpose*)
3. a word that has an *e* (*never, purpose*)
4. a word that is a synonym for *end* or *goal* (*purpose*)

Second Set:

1. a word that has an *o* (*got, fiction, nonfiction, purpose*)
2. a word that has at least one tall letter (*got, fiction, nonfiction*)
3. a word that ends with -*tion* (*fiction, nonfiction*)
4. a word that has a prefix that means "not" (*nonfiction*)

Third Set:

1. a word that refers to something you could read (*fiction, nonfiction, fable*)
2. a word that means "a type of text that is not based on truth or fact" (*fiction, fable*)
3. a word that starts with an *f* (*fiction, fable*)
4. a word that rhymes with *table* (*fable*)

Fourth Set:

1. a word that has a letter that comes before *h* in the alphabet (*got, never, sequential, fiction, nonfiction, fable, purpose*)
2. a word that has fewer than 10 letters (*got, never, fiction, fable, purpose*)
3. a word that has a letter that goes below the line (*got, purpose*)
4. a word that rhymes with *hotshot* (*got*)

Stump the Class

Give pairs or small groups time to work together to find relationships among this week's words. Once they have found a category into which several of the words fit, they should write the words in a circle on the Word Clusters sheet (see page 127) and the category underneath. Allow time for each pair or group to share one set of their words and ask the rest of the class to guess the category. Even though the other students may suggest a legitimate

category, only the presenters' category is the correct answer. The goal is to stump the rest of the class with a unique category. (You might discover categories that you can add to the Day 5: Word Smart activity.)

Day 3: Word Builder

Have students separate the letters at the bottom of this week's word template. Ask them to spell words as you call them out. Have students construct words based on patterns in the words and call out words in increasingly difficult order as shown below. The final word should answer this clue: Reading these will give you goosebumps. (*mysteries*)

sit	tie	rest	rim	mess
sits	ties	rests	rims	messy
set	term	steer	trim	mysteries
reset	terms	steers	trims	
rise	stem	mist	time	
rises	stems	misty	times	

As students spell each word, write it on the board. Ask them to cross-check their spelling with yours and correct any errors. On the board or in a pocket chart, sort the words according to the following spelling patterns:

-im
rim
trim

After all the words have been spelled and sorted, have students read over the list, emphasizing the spelling pattern from the first vowel to the end of each word. In the case of multisyllabic words, the rimes are a bit different, so stress the rhymes of these words.

Tell students that these patterns can help them spell many other words. The Day 4 activity will start with these patterns.

This activity lends itself well to exploring word endings. The pairs of words include one with and one without an ending. Go over the words and show how these new endings were added and how they change the meaning.

Day 4: Rhymer

Return to some of the patterns from the Day 3 lesson. With students, brainstorm a list of words using these rime patterns. This can be done in several different ways:

- The whole group brainstorms with you and makes a list.
- Assign the same or different patterns to partners or small groups. Have them create a list of words to share with the class.
- Make the small-group assignment competitive. Choose a pattern and let each group take turns adding a word to the list

until only one group is able to add a word. You might want to let groups use a dictionary to verify their words.

Day 5: Word Smart

Distribute the Lesson 17 words and ask students to arrange them across the top of their desk with plenty of workspace below. Have students respond to your questions by picking up the correct word card(s) and holding it so you can see their answer. If there are more than two correct answers, tell students to show only two—one in each hand. Ask students, "Can you find the . . ."

- word that rhymes with *table*?
- word hiding an antonym of *stop*?
- word that means "text that is based on fact and what is real"?
- word that means "text based on imagination"?
- word that is hiding what you might do when someone takes your picture?
- word hiding the word *ever*?
- word that ends with the same syllable as the word *motion*?
- word that results from 10 minus 5 plus 1?
- word that has a prefix that means "not"?
- word that is the past tense of *get*?
- word that names a type of story that Aesop wrote?
- word that describes a natural order of numbers or events?
- word that tells what authors have in mind when they write?
- word that describes "The Lion and the Mouse"?
- word that describes the book _____? (Fill in the blank with something the class has read—fiction or nonfiction.)
- word that describes the book _____? (Fill in the blank with something the class has read—fiction or nonfiction.)
- word that describes the book _____? (Fill in the blank with something the class has read—fiction or nonfiction.)
- word that could be described as "to inform" or "to entertain" in reference to a piece of writing?
- word that means "at no time"?
- word that rhymes with *sticks* but is spelled differently?

✳ Homework ✳

After Day 5, words go home with students. They review the words and use them to complete the Parent-Child Word Work page (see page 128).

Day 1: Meet the Words

Have students pull apart the 8 word cards for this lesson and arrange the cards across the top of their desk. Then ask them to do the following:

- Hold up each card as you pronounce the word on it.
- Look at the word, read it aloud, and spell it with you.
- Return the word card to the top of their desk.

Say each word. Provide a simple definition as necessary and share some of its features as described below. You may want to have students use their fingers to cover certain letters to isolate phonic elements such as initial letters, blends, vowels, or hidden words, or point to certain letters as you discuss them. Clap the syllables in each word, and use it in a sentence that helps students understand the meaning of the word.

Some notable features of these words include the following:

* **seven**: frequently-used word, especially related to math; 2 syllables; hidden word: *even*
* **eight**: frequently-used word, especially related to math; tricky spelling; same spelling pattern as *freight, weight*
* **tonight**: frequently-used word; close to spelling pattern of *eight* but different sound due to the *ei* combination in *eight*; 2 syllables; compound word; hidden words: *to, night, ton*
* **compost**: word used in science meaning "a mixture of decaying items" ("We throw all of our leftover fruits and vegetables into the compost pile in our yard."); word part *com* means "with or together"; 2 syllables; hidden word: *post*
* **organism**: any life form—plant, animal, fungus (*life* defined as something that eats, breathes, and grows—even though not necessarily as humans do); *-ism* is a suffix; 4 syllables; hidden words: *organ, or, is*
* **consumer**: multiple-meaning word (*noun*); used in social studies; related to economics: "person who buys goods or services from a company" ("You are a consumer when you buy an ice cream cone."); used in science as an organism that feeds on other plants or animals ("Cats, birds, cows, and fish are consumers that survive by eating plants, organisms, and other animals."); explore how the definitions relate to each other; *-er* suffix changes verb, *consume*, into noun—a person who consumes; 3 syllables; hidden words: *on, sum, me, con*
* **producer**: multiple-meaning word (*noun*); used in social studies; related to economics: "person or company that makes goods to be sold" ("Your favorite company is a producer of fast food."); used in science as an organism that makes its own food, such as a plant that survives on air, soil, and light; also means "someone who makes a film, movie, video, or music"; explore how the definitions relate to each other; *-er* suffix

changes verb, *produce*, into noun—"a person who produces"; 3 syllables; hidden words: *pro, produce, rod*

* **decomposer**: word used in science meaning "an organism that eats, breaks down, or decomposes matter (dead plants and animals)"; prefix *de-* means "against or to do the opposite" (a composer puts things together, and a decomposer does just the opposite); suffix *-er* changes the base word from a verb to a noun; word part *com* means "with or together"; 4 syllables; hidden word: *pose*

Compare the *-er* suffix in all 3 words: *consumer, producer, decomposer*; *-er* changes the base word into someone or something who does some action.

Day 2: Word Whittle

Distribute the plastic bags containing this week's words or ask students to retrieve them. Have students place the words across the top of their workspace. After you read the first clue, they pull down all the words that fit it. For each subsequent clue in the set, students continue to whittle the words by returning those that don't fit to the top of their workspace. No new words can be added to the group after the first clue. Only one word will remain after the final clue in a set. Students return the word card to the top of their workspace before the next set of clues begins.

First Set:

1. a word that has more than 2 syllables (*organism, consumer, producer, decomposer*)
2. a word that has a suffix (*organism, consumer, producer, decomposer*)
3. a word that has at least 3 vowels (*organism, consumer, producer, decomposer*)
4. a word that could describe the other 3 words (*organism*)

Second Set:

1. a word that starts with a letter that comes before *m* in the alphabet (*eight, compost, consumer, decomposer*)
2. a word that has a tall letter (*eight, compost, decomposer*)
3. a word that ends with a /t/ sound (*eight, compost*)
4. a word that means "a mixture of decaying matter" (*compost*)

Third Set:

1. a word that has 2 syllables (*seven, tonight, compost*)
2. a word that has 2 vowels (*seven, tonight, compost*)
3. a word that has letters that extend above or below the line (*tonight, compost*)
4. a word that is a compound (*tonight*)

Fourth Set:

1. a word that has fewer than 8 letters (*seven, eight, tonight, compost*)

2. a word that has 2 vowels (*seven, eight, tonight, compost*)
3. a word that names a number (*seven, eight*)
4. a word that rhymes with *weight* (*eight*)

Stump the Class

Give pairs or small groups time to work together to find relationships among this week's words. Once they have found a category into which several of the words fit, they should write the words in a circle on the Word Clusters sheet (see page 127) and the category underneath. Allow time for each pair or group to share one set of their words and ask the rest of the class to guess the category. Even though the other students may suggest a legitimate category, only the presenters' category is the correct answer. The goal is to stump the rest of the class with a unique category. (You might discover categories that you can add to the Day 5: Word Smart activity.)

Day 3: Word Builder

Have students separate the letters at the bottom of this week's word template. Ask them to spell words as you call them out. Have students construct words based on patterns in the words and call out words in increasingly difficult order as shown below. The final word should answer this clue: It can be long and wiggly, or so tiny you can't see it. (*decomposer*)

sore	poem	room	code
score	poems	doom	mode
coop	rose	some	rope
scoop	pose	come	mope
scooped	compose	mop	decompose
	composer	cop	decomposer
		drop	

As students spell each word, write it on the board. Ask them to cross-check their spelling with yours and correct any errors. On the board or in a pocket chart, sort the words according to the following spelling patterns:

-oop	-oom	-ome	-op	-ode	-ope
coop	room	some	mop	code	rope
scoop	doom	come	cop	mode	mope
			drop		

After all the words have been spelled and sorted, have students read over the list, emphasizing the spelling pattern from the first vowel to the end of each word. In the case of multisyllabic words, the rimes are a bit different, so stress the rhymes of these words. Tell students that these patterns can help them spell many other words. The Day 4 activity will start with these patterns. Take an opportunity to talk about some of the following elements: *-er* and *-ed* endings.

Day 4: Rhymer

Return to some of the patterns from the Day 3 lesson. With students, brainstorm a list of words using these rime patterns. This can be done in several different ways:
- The whole group brainstorms with you and makes a list.

- Assign the same or different patterns to partners or small groups. Have them create a list of words to share with the class.
- Make the small-group assignment competitive. Choose a pattern and let each group take turns adding a word to the list until only one group is able to add a word. You might want to let groups use a dictionary to verify their words.

Day 5: Word Smart

Distribute the Lesson 18 words and ask students to arrange them across the top of their desk with plenty of workspace below. Have students respond to your questions by picking up the correct word card(s) and holding it so you can see their answer. If there are more than two correct answers, tell students to show only two—one in each hand. Ask students, "Can you find the . . ."

- word that rhymes with *Kate* and *freight*?
- word that names a number? a time?
- word that is hiding something you might hear played in church?
- word that is hiding something you get when you add numbers?
- word that rhymes with *eleven*? *bright*?
- word that means "someone who shops and buys things"?
- word that means "a mixture of decaying matter"?
- word with a prefix that means "against or just the opposite"?
- word with a suffix that means "someone or something that does something"?

Tell students to separate these 3 words from the others: *producer, consumer, decomposer.* Have them think of the food chain. Then ask them to identify each organism below as a *producer, consumer,* or *decomposer.*

dog	cat	fish	rose	fungi
bacteria	worms	grass	mushrooms	mold
butterfly	cactus	tree	you!	

Now tell students to remove *decomposer* from the group of words. Ask them to think about economics—how money works. Have them choose which word—*producer* or *consumer*—is represented in the following scenarios:
- You buy an ice cream cone. You are a _____.
- You run a lemonade stand. You are a _____.
- You babysit for a neighbor. The neighbor is a _____, and you are a _____.

Day 1: Meet the Words

Have students pull apart the 8 word cards for this lesson and arrange the cards across the top of their desk. Then ask them to do the following:

- Hold up each card as you pronounce the word on it.
- Look at the word, read it aloud, and spell it with you.
- Return the word card to the top of their desk.

Say each word. Provide a simple definition as necessary and share some of its features as described below. You may want to have students use their fingers to cover certain letters to isolate phonic elements such as initial letters, blends, vowels, or hidden words, or point to certain letters as you discuss them. Clap the syllables in each word, and use it in a sentence that helps students understand the meaning of the word.

Some notable features of these words include the following:

* **myself**: frequently-used word; compound word; pronoun; 2 syllables; hidden words: *my, self, elf*

* **much**: frequently-used word; /ch/ sound; rhymes with *such* and also with words such as *touch* and *crutch* that have a different spelling pattern

* **keep**: frequently-used word; double vowel has a long-e sound; means "to hold or have"; -eep pattern helps spell many words, such as *asleep, jeep, sweep, steep, weep*

* **fact**: word used in many content areas, especially language arts; synonym for *truth*; opposite of *opinion* in language arts; hidden word: *act*

* **opinion**: word used in many content areas, especially language arts; means "a personal belief which may be questioned by others"; 3 syllables; hidden words: *pin, on, in*

* **angle**: word used often in math; means "the space between 2 intersecting lines; switching 2 letters changes *angle* into *angel*; 2 syllables; hidden word: *an*

* **parallel**: word used often in math; means "extending in the same direction where the distance between never changes"; prefix *para-* means "beside," as in lines beside each other that never meet; 3 syllables; hidden words: *par, all, pa*

* **perpendicular**: word used often in math; means "2 lines that intersect at right angles" ("An intersection with a stop light is often formed by two perpendicular streets."); 5 syllables; hidden word: *pen*

Day 2: Word Whittle

Distribute the plastic bags containing this week's words or ask students to retrieve them. Have students place the words across the top of their workspace. After you read the first clue, they pull down all the words that fit it. For each subsequent clue in the set, students continue to whittle the words by returning those that don't fit to the top of their workspace. No new words can be added to the group after the first clue. Only one word will remain after the final clue in a set. Students return the word card to the top of their workspace before the next set of clues begins.

First Set:

1. a word that has an *a* (*fact, angle, parallel, perpendicular*)
2. a word that has more than 1 syllable (*angle, parallel, perpendicular*)
3. a word that has to do with lines (*angle, parallel, perpendicular*)
4. a word that refers to the space between 2 intersecting lines (*angle*)

Second Set:

1. a word that has a tall letter (*myself, much, keep, fact, angle, parallel, perpendicular*)
2. a word that has at least 2 tall letters (*myself, fact, parallel, perpendicular*)
3. a word that starts with the same sound as *pencil* (*parallel, perpendicular*)
4. a word that has 5 syllables (*perpendicular*)

Third Set:

1. a word that has 1 syllable (*much, keep, fact*)
2. a word that has 1 vowel (*much, fact*)
3. a word that ends with 2 consonants (*much, fact*)
4. a word that means "truth" (*fact*)

Fourth Set:

1. a word that has at least 1 e (*myself, keep, angle, parallel, perpendicular*)
2. a word that has 2 syllables (*myself, angle*)
3. a word that has a letter that goes below the line (*myself, angle*)
4. a word that is a compound word (*myself*)

Stump the Class

Give pairs or small groups time to work together to find relationships among this week's words. Once they have found a category into which several of the words fit, they should write the words in a circle on the Word Clusters sheet (see page 127) and the category underneath. Allow time for each pair or group to share one set of their words and ask the rest of the class to guess the category. Even though the other students may suggest a legitimate

category, only the presenters' category is the correct answer. The goal is to stump the rest of the class with a unique category. (You might discover categories that you can add to the Day 5: Word Smart activity.)

Day 3: Word Builder

Have students separate the letters at the bottom of this week's word template. Ask them to spell words as you call them out. Have students construct words based on patterns in the words and call out words in increasingly difficult order as shown below. The final word should answer this clue: This is a big number word. (*mathematics*)

mat	each	ash	match
hat	east	mash	matches
chat	eat	cash	mismatch
ace	heat	team	math
case	cheat	seam	mathematics
chase	meat	steam	
	seat		

As students spell each word, write it on the board. Ask them to cross-check their spelling with yours and correct any errors. On the board or in a pocket chart, sort the words according to the following spelling patterns:

-at	-ase	-eat	-ash	-eam
mat	case	eat	ash	team
hat	chase	heat	mash	seam
chat		cheat	cash	steam
		meat		
		seat		

After all the words have been spelled and sorted, have students read over the list, emphasizing the spelling pattern from the first vowel to the end of each word. In the case of multisyllabic words, the rimes are a bit different, so stress the rhymes of these words.

Tell students that these patterns can help them spell many other words. The Day 4 activity will start with these patterns.

Take an opportunity to talk about some of the following elements: the /ch/ sound; prefix *mis-*.

Day 4: Rhymer

Return to some of the patterns from the Day 3 lesson. With students, brainstorm a list of words using these rime patterns. This can be done in several different ways:

- The whole group brainstorms with you and makes a list.
- Assign the same or different patterns to partners or small groups. Have them create a list of words to share with the class.
- Make the small-group assignment competitive. Choose a pattern and let each group take turns adding a word to the list

until only one group is able to add a word. You might want to let groups use a dictionary to verify their words.

Day 5: Word Smart

Distribute the Lesson 19 words and ask students to arrange them across the top of their desk with plenty of workspace below. Have students respond to your questions by picking up the correct word card(s) and holding it so you can see their answer. If there are more than two correct answers, tell students to show only two—one in each hand. Ask students, "Can you find the . . ."

- word that relates to math? that is a compound?
- word with a long-*e* sound?
- word that rhymes with *touch*? *exact*? *jeep*?
- word that is a synonym for *truth*?
- word that means "the space between 2 intersecting lines"?
- word that is close to being an angel?
- word that fits in this sentence: "His _____ was that the movie was too long."?
- word that has 5 syllables? 3 syllables?
- word that starts with the same sound as *Monday*?
- word that fits in this sentence: "We ate too _____ candy, and now our stomachs hurt!"?
- word that describes 2 lines with an equal distance between them that move in the same direction side by side?
- word that rhymes with *eggshell*? *asleep*?

Now have your students put the words *fact* and *opinion* in their workspace. Ask them to use these words to identify whether each of the following is a fact or opinion:

- The first president of the United States was George Washington.
- Today is a wonderful day!
- Tabitha tells funny jokes.
- _____ (principal's name) is our principal.
- Today is _____ . (day of week)
- Earth has one moon.
- Blue is the prettiest color.
- A year has 12 months.

Day 1: Meet the Words

Have students pull apart the 8 word cards for this lesson and arrange the cards across the top of their desk. Then ask them to do the following:

- Hold up each card as you pronounce the word on it.
- Look at the word, read it aloud, and spell it with you.
- Return the word card to the top of their desk.

Say each word. Provide a simple definition as necessary and share some of its features as described below. You may want to have students use their fingers to cover certain letters to isolate phonic elements such as initial letters, blends, vowels, or hidden words, or point to certain letters as you discuss them. Clap the syllables in each word, and use it in a sentence that helps students understand the meaning of the word.

Some notable features of these words include the following:

* **try**: frequently-used word; verb; *y* makes a long-*i* sound; *r*-blend; *tr*; *-y* spelling pattern also used in *by* and *my*

* **start**: frequently-used word; /st/ blend; *-art* spelling pattern used for words like *cart, outsmart, chart*; hidden words: *tart, art, star*

* **highest**: frequently-used word; base word *high* with *-igh* making long-*i* sound; suffix *-est* means "greatest degree": *high, higher, highest*; opposite of *lowest*; 2 syllables; hidden words: *hi, he, high*

* **global**: word used often in science and social studies; means "worldwide," as in "Many scientists tell us that we have a global warming pattern."; base word *globe* with *-al* suffix that means "related to globe"; 2 syllables; hidden words: *lo, lob, glob*

* **climate**: word used often in science and social studies; means "the weather conditions in a place"; *c*-blend: *cl*; 2 syllables; hidden words: *mate, ma, ate*

* **agriculture**: word used often in social studies; means "the raising of crops, livestock, or poultry"; 4 syllables; hidden word: *culture*

* **scarcity**: word used often in social studies; means "shortage," as in "When it didn't rain for months, there was a scarcity of corn in the fields."; 3 syllables; hidden words: *scar, car, city, it*

* **manufacturing**: word used often in social studies; means "making or producing by hand or machinery"; 5 syllables; hidden words: *man, fact, act, ring*

Day 2: Word Whittle

Distribute the plastic bags containing this week's words or ask students to retrieve them. Have students place the words across the top of their workspace. After you read the first clue, they pull down all the words that fit it. For each subsequent clue in the set, students continue to whittle the words by returning those that don't fit to the top of their workspace. No new words can be added to the group after the first clue. Only one word will remain after the final clue in a set. Students return the word card to the top of their workspace before the next set of clues begins.

First Set:
1. a word that has 2 syllables (*highest, global, climate*)
2. a word that has at least 2 vowels (*highest, global, climate*)
3. a word that ends with a consonant (*highest, global*)
4. a word that means "worldwide" (*global*)

Second Set:
1. a word that has more than 2 syllables (*agriculture, scarcity, manufacturing*)
2. a word that has 5 vowels (*agriculture, manufacturing*)
3. a word that starts and ends with a vowel (*agriculture*)

Third Set:
1. a word that has an *r* (*try, start, agriculture, scarcity, manufacturing*)
2. a word that has an *r* and a *t* (*try, start, agriculture, scarcity, manufacturing*)
3. a word that has 2 tall letters (*start, agriculture, manufacturing*)
4. a word that has 2 of the same tall letter (*start*)

Fourth Set:
1. a word that has an *i* (*highest, climate, agriculture, scarcity, manufacturing*)
2. a word that has a letter that goes below the line (*highest, agriculture, scarcity, manufacturing*)
3. a word that has fewer than 4 syllables (*highest, scarcity*)
4. a word that has a hidden word that means "a large town" (*scarcity*)

Stump the Class

Give pairs or small groups time to work together to find relationships among this week's words. Once they have found a category into which several of the words fit, they should write the words in a circle on the Word Clusters sheet (see page 127) and the category underneath. Allow time for each pair or group to share one set of their words and ask the rest of the class to guess the category. Even though the other students may suggest a legitimate

category, only the presenters' category is the correct answer. The goal is to stump the rest of the class with a unique category. (You might discover categories that you can add to the Day 5: Word Smart activity.)

Day 3: Word Builder

Have students separate the letters at the bottom of this week's word template. Ask them to spell words as you call them out. Have students construct words based on patterns in the words and call out words in increasingly difficult order as shown below. The final word should answer this clue: A man isn't the only one who can do this. (*manufacture*)

face	art	true	man
race	cart	untrue	fact
mace	ate	fear	manufacture
trace	rate	tear	
arm	mate	near	
farm	fate	name	
act	crate	tame	
react		fame	
		frame	

As students spell each word, write it on the board. Ask them to cross-check their spelling with yours and correct any errors. On the board or in a pocket chart, sort the words according to the following spelling patterns:

-ace	-arm	-art	-ate	-ear	-ame
face	arm	art	ate	fear	name
race	farm	cart	rate	tear	tame
mace			mate	near	fame
trace			fate		frame
			crate		

After all the words have been spelled and sorted, have students read over the list, emphasizing the spelling pattern from the first vowel to the end of each word. In the case of multisyllabic words, the rimes are a bit different, so stress the rhymes of these words.

Tell students that these patterns can help them spell many other words. The Day 4 activity will start with these patterns.

Take an opportunity to talk about some of the following elements: prefixes: *re-* (*act/react*), *un-* (*true/untrue*).

Day 4: Rhymer

Return to some of the patterns from the Day 3 lesson. With students, brainstorm a list of words using these rime patterns. This can be done in several different ways:

- The whole group brainstorms with you and makes a list.

- Assign the same or different patterns to partners or small groups. Have them create a list of words to share with the class.
- Make the small-group assignment competitive. Choose a pattern and let each group take turns adding a word to the list until only one group is able to add a word. You might want to let groups use a dictionary to verify their words.

Day 5: Word Smart

Distribute the Lesson 20 words and ask students to arrange them across the top of their desk with plenty of workspace below. Have students respond to your questions by picking up the correct word card(s) and holding it so you can see their answer. If there are more than two correct answers, tell students to show only two—one in each hand. Ask students, "Can you find the . . ."

- word that is the opposite of *finish*?
- word that is a synonym for *worldwide*?
- word that is hiding a partner?
- word that is hiding a grown boy?
- word that has 5 syllables? 2 syllables?
- word that is hiding a mark left from a cut that has healed?
- word that refers to weather conditions?
- word that fits in this sentence: "All you can do is _____ to do your best."?
- word that is hiding the opposite of *opinion*?
- word that rhymes with *chart*? *my*?
- word that starts the same as the word *stack*?
- word hiding something you wear on your finger?
- word that means "the raising of crops, livestock, or poultry"?
- word that means "producing or making products by hand or with machinery"?
- word with a suffix that compares?
- word hiding something you ride in?
- word that, if you changed the first letter, could bring big tears?
- word with 4 syllables? 1 syllable?

❈ Homework ❈

After Day 5, words go home with students. They review the words and use them to complete the Parent-Child Word Work page (see page 128).

Day 1: Meet the Words

Have students pull apart the 8 word cards for this lesson and arrange the cards across the top of their desk. Then ask them to do the following:

- Hold up each card as you pronounce the word on it.
- Look at the word, read it aloud, and spell it with you.
- Return the word card to the top of their desk.

Say each word. Provide a simple definition as necessary and share some of its features as described below. You may want to have students use their fingers to cover certain letters to isolate phonic elements such as initial letters, blends, vowels, or hidden words, or point to certain letters as you discuss them. Clap the syllables in each word, and use it in a sentence that helps students understand the meaning of the word.

Some notable features of these words include the following:

* **bring**: frequently-used word; *-ing* pattern helps spell many additional words; verb; hidden words: *ring, in*

* **drink**: frequently-used word; *-ink* pattern helps spell many additional words, such as *think, stink, link, wink*; verb; hidden words: *rink, ink, in*

* **only**: frequently-used word; *-ly* sometimes signals adverb usage, but this is both adverb and adjective; 2 syllables; hidden word: *on*

* **declarative**: word used often in language arts; describes a sentence that makes a statement, also called a "telling" sentence; *-ative* ending changes *declare* (verb) into an adjective; 4 syllables; hidden words: *rat, at*

* **exclamatory**: word used often in language arts; describes a sentence that shows strong emotion or surprise; base word is *exclaim* (verb) with ending that changes it to an adjective; an exclamatory sentence uses an exclamation point for its ending; 5 syllables; hidden words: *clam, ma, mat*

* **orbit**: word used often in science for the curved path that one celestial body takes around another larger body, such as a moon around a planet or a planet around the sun; Earth's orbit around the sun along with the tilt of Earth causes our seasons; 2 syllables; hidden words: *or, orb, it*

* **solar**: word used often in science; means "related to the sun"; comes from *sol* which means "sun"; 2 syllables; *r*-controlled ending, so do not forget the *a*; hidden word: *so*

* **rotation**: word used often in science to describe how celestial bodies spin as they complete their orbit; Earth's rotation creates our days and nights; hidden words: *rot, ion, on*

Day 2: Word Whittle

Distribute the plastic bags containing this week's words or ask students to retrieve them. Have students place the words across the top of their workspace. After you read the first clue, they pull down all the words that fit it. For each subsequent clue in the set, students continue to whittle the words by returning those that don't fit to the top of their workspace. No new words can be added to the group after the first clue. Only one word will remain after the final clue in a set. Students return the word card to the top of their workspace before the next set of clues begins.

First Set:

1. a word that has 2 syllables (*only, orbit, solar*)
2. a word that has 5 letters (*orbit, solar*)
3. a word that has 2 vowels (*orbit, solar*)
4. a word that means "something related to the sun" (*solar*)

Second Set:

1. a word that has more than 2 syllables (*declarative, exclamatory, rotation*)
2. a word that has a vowel as its second letter (*declarative, rotation*)
3. a word with tall letters (*declarative, rotation*)
4. a word that describes a sentence that makes a statement (*declarative*)

Third Set:

1. a word with no more than 5 letters (*bring, drink, only, orbit, solar*)
2. a word that has an *i* (*bring, drink, orbit*)
3. a word that starts with a consonant (*bring, drink*)
4. a word that rhymes with *spring* (*bring*)

Fourth Set:

1. a word that relates to the study of the stars and planets (*orbit, solar, rotation*)
2. a word that relates to movement of celestial bodies (*orbit, rotation*)
3. a word that has 2 tall letters (*orbit, rotation*)
4. a word that means "a curved path followed by a celestial body such as Earth" (*orbit*)

Stump the Class

Give pairs or small groups time to work together to find relationships among this week's words. Once they have found a category into which several of the words fit, they should write the words in a circle on the Word Clusters sheet (see page 127) and the category underneath. Allow time for each pair or group to share one set of their words and ask the rest of the class to guess the category. Even though the other students may suggest a legitimate category, only the presenters' category is the correct answer. The goal is to stump the rest of the class with a unique category. (You might discover categories that you can add to the Day 5: Word Smart activity.)

Day 3: Word Builder

Have students separate the letters at the bottom of this week's word template. Ask them to spell words as you call them out. Have students construct words based on patterns in the words and call out words in increasingly difficult order as shown below. The final word should answer this clue: This is the study of the stars. (*astronomy*)

any	arm	say	Mars	rosy	storm
many	army	May	mart	nosy	stormy
may	toy	tray	smart	story	astronomy
mayor	toys	stay			

As students spell each word, write it on the board. Ask them to cross-check their spelling with yours and correct any errors. On the board or in a pocket chart, sort the words according to the following spelling patterns:

-any	-ay	-art	-osy
any	say	mart	rosy
many	May	smart	nosy
	tray		
	stay		

After all the words have been spelled and sorted, have students read over the list, emphasizing the spelling pattern from the first vowel to the end of each word. In the case of multisyllabic words, the rimes are a bit different, so stress the rhymes of these words.

Tell students that these patterns can help them spell many other words. The Day 4 activity will start with these patterns.

Take an opportunity to talk about some of the following elements: word part *ast* means "star" (*aster, astronomy, astronaut*); -*y* ending changes meaning of words (*rose/rosy, nose/nosy, storm/stormy*).

Day 4: Rhymer

Return to some of the patterns from the Day 3 lesson. With students, brainstorm a list of words using these rime patterns. This can be done in several different ways:

- The whole group brainstorms with you and makes a list.
- Assign the same or different patterns to partners or small groups. Have them create a list of words to share with the class.
- Make the small-group assignment competitive. Choose a

pattern and let each group take turns adding a word to the list until only one group is able to add a word. You might want to let groups use a dictionary to verify their words.

Day 5: Word Smart

Distribute the Lesson 21 words and ask students to arrange them across the top of their desk with plenty of workspace below. Have students respond to your questions by picking up the correct word card(s) and holding it so you can see their answer. If there are more than two correct answers, tell students to show only two—one in each hand. Ask students, "Can you find the . . ."

- word that rhymes with *fling*? *sink*?
- word that has 5 syllables?
- word that has 2 syllables?
- word hiding something that flows from a pen to a piece of paper?
- word that relates to the sun?
- word that deals with the movement of a celestial body?
- word that fits in this sentence: "I can _____ do one thing at a time."?
- word that describes a sentence that makes a statement, a telling sentence?
- word that describes a sentence that shows emotion or surprise?
- word that refers to something turning round and round?
- word hiding a synonym for *decay*?
- word that hides the name of something you skate around?
- word hiding a small spherical shape?

Now have students put the words *exclamatory* and *declarative* in their workspace. Ask them to show the correct word that identifies each of the following sentences:

- Hurry! Grab the papers that are blowing away!
- Today we will study the solar system.
- Earth is nearly twice the size of Mars.
- What an amazing picture of our solar system!
- The dog has eaten the sofa pillows!
- Let's walk to the park.

❋ Homework ❋

After Day 5, words go home with students. They review the words and use them to complete the Parent-Child Word Work page (see page 128).

Day 1: Meet the Words

Have students pull apart the 8 word cards for this lesson and arrange the cards across the top of their desk. Then ask them to do the following:

- Hold up each card as you pronounce the word on it.
- Look at the word, read it aloud, and spell it with you.
- Return the word card to the top of their desk.

Say each word. Provide a simple definition as necessary and share some of its features as described below. You may want to have students use their fingers to cover certain letters to isolate phonic elements such as initial letters, blends, vowels, or hidden words, or point to certain letters as you discuss them. Clap the syllables in each word, and use it in a sentence that helps students understand the meaning of the word.

Some notable features of these words include the following:

✳ **better**: frequently-used word; most often used as an adjective; double consonant; 2 syllables; hidden words: *bet, be*

✳ **hold**: frequently-used word; often used as a verb; *-old* spelling pattern helps spell words such as *bold, cold, scold, mold, fold*; hidden word: *old*

✳ **warm**: frequently-used word; adjective ("This is a warm dish.") or verb ("Please warm this dish before putting it on the table."); tricky *a*—be careful!; hidden word: *arm*

✳ **interrogative**: used often in language arts to describe a sentence that asks a question; relate to *interrogate* where you ask someone many questions; prefix *inter-* means "between," which refers to someone asking and someone answering a question; *-tive* suffix usually means a word is an adjective; 5 syllables; hidden words: *in, err*

✳ **imperative**: used often in language arts to describe a sentence that gives a command, such as "Get me that pencil." or "Turn left at the corner."; also used to mean that something is vitally important, as in "Looking both ways before crossing the street is imperative for your safety!"; *-tive* suffix usually means a word is an adjective; 4 syllables; hidden words: *era, rat, at, imp*

✳ **quart**: word used often in math; base word translates to mean "fourth"; in math, means "a liquid measurement of 1/4 gallon" (*4 quarts = 1 gallon*); relates to *quarter*, which is 1/4 of a dollar, and *quartet*, which is a group of 4 singers or musicians; the letter *q* is almost always followed by the letter *u*; hidden word: *art*

✳ **pound**: word used often in math; a unit of measure of weight that equals 16 ounces; multiple meaning: (*verb*) "to hit something repeatedly," and (*noun*) "a place where homeless pets are kept"; abbreviation, oddly enough, is *lb.*; *-ound* spelling pattern helps spell words such as *sound, mound, ground*; /ou/ sound

✳ **ounce**: word used often in math; a unit of measurement which equals 1/16 of a pound; abbreviation is *oz*; spelling pattern helps spell words such as *pounce, flounce, trounce*; /ou/ sound

Day 2: Word Whittle

Distribute the plastic bags containing this week's words or ask students to retrieve them. Have students place the words across the top of their workspace. After you read the first clue, they pull down all the words that fit it. For each subsequent clue in the set, students continue to whittle the words by returning those that don't fit to the top of their workspace. No new words can be added to the group after the first clue. Only one word will remain after the final clue in a set. Students return the word card to the top of their workspace before the next set of clues begins.

First Set:
1. a word that has 1 syllable (*hold, warm, quart, pound, ounce*)
2. a word that has a tall letter (*hold, quart, pound*)
3. a word that names a measurement (*quart, pound*)
4. a word that fits in this sentence: "There is 1 _____ of milk left." (*quart*)

Second Set:
1. a word that has more than 1 syllable (*better, interrogative, imperative*)
2. a word that has more than 2 vowels (*interrogative, imperative*)
3. a word that ends with a *-tive* suffix (*interrogative, imperative*)
4. a word that has 5 syllables (*interrogative*)

Third Set:
1. a word that has fewer than 7 letters (*better, hold, warm, quart, pound, ounce*)
2. a word that has a vowel for its second letter (*better, hold, warm, quart, pound, ounce*)
3. a word that starts with a tall letter (*better, hold*)
4. a word that fits in this sentence: "I would make a _____ grade if I studied harder." (*better*)

Fourth Set:
1. a word that begins and ends with a consonant (*better, hold, warm, quart, pound*)
2. a word that has only 1 vowel (*hold, warm*)
3. a word that has just 4 letters (*hold, warm*)
4. a word that rhymes with *scold* (*hold*)

Stump the Class
Give pairs or small groups time to work together to find relationships among this week's words. Once they have found a

category into which several of the words fit, they should write the words in a circle on the Word Clusters sheet (see page 127) and the category underneath. Allow time for each pair or group to share one set of their words and ask the rest of the class to guess the category. Even though the other students may suggest a legitimate category, only the presenters' category is the correct answer. The goal is to stump the rest of the class with a unique category. (You might discover categories that you can add to the Day 5: Word Smart activity.)

Day 3: Word Builder

Have students separate the letters at the bottom of this week's word template. Ask them to spell words as you call them out. Have students construct words based on patterns in the words and call out words in increasingly difficult order as shown below. The final word should answer this clue: This is measured in ounces, but it can put pounds on your body! (*hamburgers*)

mug	gum	rush	game	ham
smug	hum	mush	same	sham
rug	sum	brush	arm	burger
shrug	sag	mash	harm	hamburgers
	bag	bash	Mars	
	brag		bars	

As students spell each word, write it on the board. Ask them to cross-check their spelling with yours and correct any errors. On the board or in a pocket chart, sort the words according to the following spelling patterns:

-ug	-um	-ag	-ush	-ash	-arm	-ars
mug	gum	sag	rush	mash	arm	Mars
smug	hum	bag	mush	bash	harm	bars
rug	sum	brag	brush			
shrug						

After all the words have been spelled and sorted, have students read over the list, emphasizing the spelling pattern from the first vowel to the end of each word. In the case of multisyllabic words, the rimes are a bit different, so stress the rhymes of these words.

Tell students that these patterns can help them spell many other words. The Day 4 activity will start with these patterns.

Day 4: Rhymer

Return to some of the patterns from the Day 3 lesson. With students, brainstorm a list of words using these rime patterns. This can be done in several different ways:

- The whole group brainstorms with you and makes a list.
- Assign the same or different patterns to partners or small groups. Have them create a list of words to share with the class.

- Make the small-group assignment competitive. Choose a pattern and let each group take turns adding a word to the list until only one group is able to add a word. You might want to let groups use a dictionary to verify their words.

Day 5: Word Smart

Distribute the Lesson 22 words and ask students to arrange them across the top of their desk with plenty of workspace below. Have students respond to your questions by picking up the correct word card(s) and holding it so you can see their answer. If there are more than two correct answers, tell students to show only two—one in each hand. Ask students, "Can you find the . . ."

- word that names a kind of sentence? a measurement?
- word that means "16 ounces"? "1/4 of a gallon"?
- word that is abbreviated *oz*?
- word that rhymes with *fold*? *pounce*?
- word that has the little word *art*?
- word that is abbreviated *lb*?
- word that has a double consonant?
- word that starts and ends with a vowel?
- word that has the word *era* hidden in it?
- word that means "to hit something over and over again"?
- word between *hot* and *cold*?
- word that has a suffix that means "between"?
- word hiding the word *bet*? hiding a rodent?

Now have students put the words *interrogatory* and *imperative* in their workspace. Ask them to identify each type of the following sentences as you share them:

- Do you have a quart of milk?
- Fetch the stick, Rover.
- Turn left when you get to the stop sign.
- Don't go near the street.
- What time does the movie start?
- Does a pound have 16 ounces?

❈ Homework ❈

After Day 5, words go home with students. They review the words and use them to complete the Parent-Child Word Work page (see page 128).

Day 1: Meet the Words

Have students pull apart the 8 word cards for this lesson and arrange the cards across the top of their desk. Then ask them to do the following:

- Hold up each card as you pronounce the word on it.
- Look at the word, read it aloud, and spell it with you.
- Return the word card to the top of their desk.

Say each word. Provide a simple definition as necessary and share some of its features as described below. You may want to have students use their fingers to cover certain letters to isolate phonic elements such as initial letters, blends, vowels, or hidden words, or point to certain letters as you discuss them. Clap the syllables in each word, and use it in a sentence that helps students understand the meaning of the word.

Some notable features of these words include the following:

- **full**: frequently-used word; when added as a suffix, there's only one *l*, as in *thankful* and *stressful*; *-ull* spelling pattern helps spell words such as *bull* and *pull*; adjective

- **done**: frequently-used word; verb (*do*); slightly different pronunciation from other *-one* words such as *tone, bone, cone*; hidden words: *do, on, one*

- **light**: frequently-used word; also a word used in science that means "a form of energy detected with the eyes"; light travels in a straight line; *-ight* spelling pattern is a tricky one but helps to spell words such as *bright, fight, flight, might*; the digraph *gh* is silent

- **culture**: word used often in social studies to mean the beliefs, customs, and behaviors of a social, ethnic, or age group, such as "Fast food is a part of American culture."; also refers to the qualities of a person, such as manners and behavior; 2 syllables; hidden word: *cult*

- **ancestor**: word used often in social studies that means "the person from whom someone has descended," as in "Abraham Lincoln was Ben's ancestor–his great-great-great grandfather."; 3 syllables; hidden words: *an, to, or*

- **ethnic**: word used often in social studies that is an adjective referring to a characteristic shared by a group of people with the same culture ("The ethnic backgrounds of the students in this class are diverse."); 2 syllables

- **population**: word used often in social studies; means "the total number of people living in a certain area"; *-tion* shows that word is a noun; word part *pop* means "people": *popular, populate*; 4 syllables; hidden words: *pop, at*

- **artifact**: word used often in social studies; means "any object made by a human that reflects its culture" ("The artifact was a weapon made by attaching a sharpened rock to a stick."); word part *art* means "skill"; word part *fac/t* means "make or do," as in *factory* and *manufacture*; word parts together mean "made by a person's skill"; 3 syllables; hidden words: *art, fact, act, if*

Day 2: Word Whittle

Distribute the plastic bags containing this week's words or ask students to retrieve them. Have students place the words across the top of their workspace. After you read the first clue, they pull down all the words that fit it. For each subsequent clue in the set, students continue to whittle the words by returning those that don't fit to the top of their workspace. No new words can be added to the group after the first clue. Only one word will remain after the final clue in a set. Students return the word card to the top of their workspace before the next set of clues begins.

First Set:

1. a word that has 1 syllable (*full, done, light*)
2. a word that begins and ends with a consonant (*full, light*)
3. a word that has at least 2 tall letters (*full, light*)
4. a word that rhymes with *flight* (*light*)

Second Set:

1. a word that has more than 2 syllables (*ancestor, population, artifact*)
2. a word that starts with a vowel (*ancestor, artifact*)
3. a word that has a *t* (*ancestor, artifact*)
4. a word that describes a relative (*ancestor*)

Third Set:

1. a word that starts with one of the first 5 letters of the alphabet (*done, culture, ancestor, ethnic, artifact*)
2. a word that starts with a vowel (*ancestor, ethnic, artifact*)
3. a word that has 3 syllables (*ancestor, artifact*)
4. a word that is something made by a human that tells about his or her culture (*artifact*)

Fourth Set:

1. a word that relates to people in some way (*culture, ancestor, ethnic, population, artifact*)
2. a word that starts with a vowel (*ancestor, ethnic, artifact*)
3. a word that has a tall letter (*ancestor, ethnic, artifact*)
4. a word that ends the same as the word *picnic* (*ethnic*)

Stump the Class

Give pairs or small groups time to work together to find relationships among this week's words. Once they have found a category into which several of the words fit, they should write the

words in a circle on the Word Clusters sheet (see page 127) and the category underneath. Allow time for each pair or group to share one set of their words and ask the rest of the class to guess the category. Even though the other students may suggest a legitimate category, only the presenters' category is the correct answer. The goal is to stump the rest of the class with a unique category. (You might discover categories that you can add to the Day 5: Word Smart activity.)

Day 3: Word Builder

Have students separate the letters at the bottom of this week's word template. Ask them to spell words as you call them out. Have students construct words based on patterns in the words and call out words in increasingly difficult order as shown below. The final word should answer this clue: This comes in all shapes and sizes. (*population*)

tap	nail	pool	ant	tulip
pat	pail	tool	aunt	pupil
tip	tail	piano	auto	population
pit	pain	patio	until	
top	plain	out	unlit	
pop		pout	lip	

As students spell each word, write it on the board. Ask them to cross-check their spelling with yours and correct any errors. On the board or in a pocket chart, sort the words according to the following spelling patterns:

-op	-ail	-ain	-ool	-out
top	nail	pain	pool	out
pop	pail	plain	tool	pout
	tail			

After all the words have been spelled and sorted, have students read over the list, emphasizing the spelling pattern from the first vowel to the end of each word. In the case of multisyllabic words, the rimes are a bit different, so stress the rhymes of these words.

Tell students that these patterns can help them spell many other words. The Day 4 activity will start with these patterns.

Take an opportunity to talk about the following element: homophones (*ant/aunt*).

Day 4: Rhymer

Return to some of the patterns from the Day 3 lesson. With students, brainstorm a list of words using these rime patterns. This can be done in several different ways:

- The whole group brainstorms with you and makes a list.

- Assign the same or different patterns to partners or small groups. Have them create a list of words to share with the class.

- Make the small-group assignment competitive. Choose a pattern and let each group take turns adding a word to the list until only one group is able to add a word. You might want to let groups use a dictionary to verify their words.

Day 5: Word Smart

Distribute the Lesson 23 words and ask students to arrange them across the top of their desk with plenty of workspace below. Have students respond to your questions by picking up the correct word card(s) and holding it so you can see their answer. If there are more than two correct answers, tell students to show only two—one in each hand. Ask students, "Can you find the . . ."

- word that means the opposite of *empty*?
- word that is an antonym for *dark*?
- word hiding the number that comes before 2?
- word that rhymes with *bright*?
- word that refers to your grandparent, great-grandparent, or great-great grandparent?
- word that, if you changed the first letter to a *v*, would be a bird that eats dead animals?
- word that is an antonym for *shadow*?
- word hiding the main difference between fiction and nonfiction?
- word that describes the moon when we see the sunlight on its entire surface that faces Earth?
- word that ends like *picture*?
- word hiding something movie stars do?
- word that describes how we like cookies and homework to be?
- word that sounds like, but isn't spelled like, *wool*?
- word that means "the total number of people in an area"?
- word that travels in a straight line?
- word that can describe a tool, a machine, or dinnerware?
- word that refers to the behavior, customs, and beliefs of a group of people?

✳ Homework ✳

After Day 5, words go home with students. They review the words and use them to complete the Parent-Child Word Work page (see page 128).

Day 1: Meet the Words

Have students pull apart the 8 word cards for this lesson and arrange the cards across the top of their desk. Then ask them to do the following:

- Hold up each card as you pronounce the word on it.
- Look at the word, read it aloud, and spell it with you.
- Return the word card to the top of their desk.

Say each word. Provide a simple definition as necessary and share some of its features as described below. You may want to have students use their fingers to cover certain letters to isolate phonic elements such as initial letters, blends, vowels, or hidden words, or point to certain letters as you discuss them. Clap the syllables in each word, and use it in a sentence that helps students understand the meaning of the word.

Some notable features of these words include the following:

❋ **pick**: frequently-used word; verb; -ick pattern helps spell words such as *quick, stick, Nick*

❋ **cut**: frequently-used word; multiple meanings as verb ("He cut the ad out of the newspaper." or noun ("We couldn't get the cut to stop bleeding."); -ut spelling pattern helps spell words such as *hut, nut, gut, doughnut*

❋ **hurt**: frequently-used word; tricky, as /ur/ sound is also made by er and ir; -urt spelling pattern helps spell words such as *yogurt, spurt, blurt*

❋ **poetry**: word used often in language arts as one of the major text genres usually characterized by short lines put together in *rhythm* or *rhyme*, or both, chosen for their beautiful sound and meaning; word part *poet* is the person who writes poetry; 3 syllables; hidden words: *poet, try*

❋ **stanza**: word used often in language arts as one of the characteristics of poetry that is a grouping of lines usually set off by white space; 2 syllables; hidden words: *tan, an*

❋ **endangered**: word used often in science to mean "a species that is threatened with extinction"; can also be used to mean "anything that is threatened" ("The miners lives are endangered, but we hope to free them."); prefix en- means "into," as in "into danger"; 3 syllables; hidden words: *danger, anger, an, end*

❋ **predator**: word used often in science to mean "an organism that survives by eating another organism"; word part *pred* stems from *prey* and added to the -or suffix translates as "one who preys"; 3 syllables; hidden words: *red, at, or*

❋ **prey**: word used often in science to mean either (*noun*) "an animal that is hunted for food" ("The fish were easy prey for the bear.") or (*verb*) "to hunt or seize an animal" ("The bear preyed on the fish."); homophone of *pray*, which has very different meaning

Day 2: Word Whittle

Distribute the plastic bags containing this week's words or ask students to retrieve them. Have students place the words across the top of their workspace. After you read the first clue, they pull down all the words that fit it. For each subsequent clue in the set, students continue to whittle the words by returning those that don't fit to the top of their workspace. No new words can be added to the group after the first clue. Only one word will remain after the final clue in a set. Students return the word card to the top of their workspace before the next set of clues begins.

First Set:
1. a word that has a *t* (*cut, hurt, poetry, stanza, predator*)
2. a word that has 3 syllables (*poetry, predator*)
3. a word that has both a *p* and a *t* (*poetry, predator*)
4. a word that names something that has either rhyme or rhythm or both (*poetry*)

Second Set:
1. a word that has 1 syllable (*pick, cut, hurt, prey*)
2. a word that has a vowel as its second letter (*pick, cut, hurt*)
3. a word that ends with a *t* (*cut, hurt*)
4. a word that rhymes with *squirt* (*hurt*)

Third Set:
1. a science word that deals with animals (*endangered, predator, prey*)
2. a word with 3 syllables (*endangered, predator*)
3. a crocodile can be this (*endangered, predator*)
4. a word that means "something soon may not exist" (*endangered*)

Fourth Set:
1. a word that has at least 2 vowels (*poetry, stanza, endangered, predator*)
2. a word that has a *t* (*poetry, stanza, predator*)
3. a word that deals with something written (*poetry, stanza*)
4. a word that means "lines written in groups with white space around them" (*stanza*)

Stump the Class

Give pairs or small groups time to work together to find relationships among this week's words. Once they have found a category into which several of the words fit, they should write the words in a circle on the Word Clusters sheet (see page 127) and the category underneath. Allow time for each pair or group to share one set of their words and ask the rest of the class to guess the category. Even though the other students may suggest a legitimate category, only the presenters' category is the correct answer. The goal is to stump the rest of the class with a unique category. (You might discover categories that you can add to the Day 5: Word Smart activity.)

Day 3: Word Builder

Have students separate the letters at the bottom of this week's word template. Ask them to spell words as you call them out. Have students construct words based on patterns in the words and call out words in increasingly difficult order as shown below. The final word should answer this clue: These animals were once on the endangered species list. (*alligators*)

all	gill	solar	girl
tall	gills	roast	girls
gall	lots	sit	air
roll	lost	lit	stair
toll		grit	gators
goal		slit	alligators

As students spell each word, write it on the board. Ask them to cross-check their spelling with yours and correct any errors. On the board or in a pocket chart, sort the words according to the following spelling patterns:

-all	-oll	-oast	-it	-air
all	roll	roast	sit	air
tall	toll		lit	stair
gall			grit	
			slit	

After all the words have been spelled and sorted, have students read over the list, emphasizing the spelling pattern from the first vowel to the end of each word. In the case of multisyllabic words, the rimes are a bit different, so stress the rhymes of these words.

Tell students that these patterns can help them spell many other words. The Day 4 activity will start with these patterns.

Take an opportunity to talk about some of the following elements: same spelling pattern but different sound pattern in *roll, toll, goal*; alligators were once endangered, and there are many endangered animals to research.

Day 4: Rhymer

Return to some of the patterns from the Day 3 lesson. With students, brainstorm a list of words using these rime patterns. This can be done in several different ways:

- The whole group brainstorms with you and makes a list.
- Assign the same or different patterns to partners or small groups. Have them create a list of words to share with the class.

- Make the small-group assignment competitive. Choose a pattern and let each group take turns adding a word to the list until only one group is able to add a word. You might want to let groups use a dictionary to verify their words.

Day 5: Word Smart

Distribute the Lesson 24 words and ask students to arrange them across the top of their desk with plenty of workspace below. Have students respond to your questions by picking up the correct word card(s) and holding it so you can see their answer. If there are more than two correct answers, tell students to show only two—one in each hand. Ask students, "Can you find the . . ."

- word that rhymes with *day*?
- word hiding a word that means "risk"?
- word hiding something you might get from staying out in the sun?
- word that has 3 syllables?
- word that is longest in this lesson? shortest?
- word that describes what you might do to strawberries?
- word that contains its writer?
- word that has a color inside?
- word hiding the opposite of *begin*?
- word that is a homophone for what people in a church might do?
- word hiding an emotion that means you're mad?
- word that means "injured"?
- word that means that an animal survives by killing another animal?
- word that names an animal that is necessary to the survival of another animal?
- word with 1 syllable and that starts with a *p*?

Have students isolate *predator* and *prey* and use the words to answer the following questions:

- bear and fish: The bear is the _____.
- bug and frog: The frog is the _____.
- hawk and squirrel: The squirrel is the _____.
- tiger and zebra: The tiger is the _____.
- cat and mouse: The mouse is the _____.
- alligator and fish: The fish is the _____.
- fox and rabbit: The fox is the _____.

✳ Homework ✳

After Day 5, words go home with students. They review the words and use them to complete the Parent-Child Word Work page (see page 128).

Day 1: Meet the Words

Have students pull apart the 8 word cards for this lesson and arrange the cards across the top of their desk. Then ask them to do the following:

- Hold up each card as you pronounce the word on it.
- Look at the word, read it aloud, and spell it with you.
- Return the word card to the top of their desk.

Say each word. Provide a simple definition as necessary and share some of its features as described below. You may want to have students use their fingers to cover certain letters to isolate phonic elements such as initial letters, blends, vowels, or hidden words, or point to certain letters as you discuss them. Clap the syllables in each word, and use it in a sentence that helps students understand the meaning of the word.

Some notable features of these words include the following:

* **kind**: frequently-used word; *-ind* spelling pattern helps spell words such as *mind, hind, grind*; hidden words: *kin, in*
* **enough**: frequently-used word; *-ough* spelling pattern used for words such as *rough, cough, slough*; *gh* makes an /f/ sound; 2 syllables; hidden word: *no*
* **Internet**: general academic word related to technology; Internet is the largest of the interconnected networks; prefix *inter-* means "between," as in "between computers"; 3 syllables; hidden words: *in, net, tern, intern*
* **reliable**: academic word used often in connection with research; means "honest and accurate," as in "How do you know if the information in your paper is reliable?"; adjective formed from base word (*verb*) *rely* by changing the *y* to *i* and adding *-able*; *-able* is a suffix that means "capable of"; 4 syllables; hidden word: *able*
* **citation**: academic word used often in connection with research; means "the mention (written or spoken) of the source from which information has come"; citations are usually included at the end of a written piece in a bibliography; base word *cite* (verb) means "to show where information came from," as in "I will cite the quote that I'm using in my research paper."; 3 syllables; hidden words: *at, it*
* **keyboard**: academic word used most often in connection with technology; means "the row or set of keys on a piano, typewriter, phone, or computer which operates that device"; compound word; 2 syllables; hidden words: *key, boar, board, boa*
* **mouse**: academic word used most often in connection with technology; means "a small device, usually connected to a computer, that is controlled by the user to move the cursor on the screen"; multiple meaning—also names a small, furry rodent; *-ouse* spelling pattern helps with words such as *house, louse, douse*; hidden words: *use, us*
* **source**: academic word used most often related to research; means "a place from which to obtain information"; source is reported in a citation; /ô/ is tricky; hidden words: *sour, our, so*

Day 2: Word Whittle

Distribute the plastic bags containing this week's words or ask students to retrieve them. Have students place the words across the top of their workspace. After you read the first clue, they pull down all the words that fit it. For each subsequent clue in the set, students continue to whittle the words by returning those that don't fit to the top of their workspace. No new words can be added to the group after the first clue. Only one word will remain after the final clue in a set. Students return the word card to the top of their workspace before the next set of clues begins.

First Set:

1. a word that has an *i* (*kind, Internet, reliable, citation*)
2. a word that has 3 syllables (*Internet, citation*)
3. a word that has 2 *f*'s (*Internet, citation*)
4. a word that names something you would use to get information (*Internet*)

Second Set:

1. a word that has 1 syllable (*kind, mouse, source*)
2. a word that begins with a consonant (*kind, mouse, source*)
3. a word that ends with a vowel (*mouse, source*)
4. a word that rhymes with *house* (*mouse*)

Third Set:

1. a science word that relates to getting information for writing a report (*Internet, citation, keyboard, mouse, source*)
2. a word that names a part of a computer (*keyboard, mouse*)
3. a word that has both an *e* and an *o* (*keyboard, mouse*)
4. a word that is a compound (*keyboard*)

Fourth Set:

1. a word that has a tall letter (*kind, enough, Internet, reliable, citation, keyboard*)
2. a word that has an *i* (*kind, Internet, reliable, citation*)
3. a word that has a suffix (*reliable, citation*)
4. a word that is a synonym of *accurate* (*reliable*)

Stump the Class

Give pairs or small groups time to work together to find relationships among this week's words. Once they have found a

category into which several of the words fit, they should write the words in a circle on the Word Clusters sheet (see page 127) and the category underneath. Allow time for each pair or group to share one set of their words and ask the rest of the class to guess the category. Even though the other students may suggest a legitimate category, only the presenters' category is the correct answer. The goal is to stump the rest of the class with a unique category. (You might discover categories that you can add to the Day 5: Word Smart activity.)

Day 3: Word Builder

Have students separate the letters at the bottom of this week's word template. Ask them to spell words as you call them out. Have students construct words based on patterns in the words and call out words in increasingly difficult order as shown below. The final word should answer this clue: Your fingers use these to find almost everything in the world. (keyboards)

bed	robe	ark	sky
bad	rake	bark	by
sad	raked	barked	dry
boy	brake	ask	bye
broke	bake	bask	key
body	baked		boards
	bakery		keyboards

As students spell each word, write it on the board. Ask them to cross-check their spelling with yours and correct any errors. On the board or in a pocket chart, sort the words according to the following spelling patterns:

-ad	-ake	-ark	-ask	-y
bad	rake	ark	ask	sky
sad	brake	bark	bask	by
	bake			dry

After all the words have been spelled and sorted, have students read over the list, emphasizing the spelling pattern from the first vowel to the end of each word. In the case of multisyllabic words, the rimes are a bit different, so stress the rhymes of these words.

Tell students that these patterns can help them spell many other words. The Day 4 activity will start with these patterns.

Take an opportunity to talk about some of the following elements: homophones (by, bye), past tense (rake/raked, bake/baked, bark/barked), endings (bake/bakery), plurals (keyboards).

Day 4: Rhymer

Return to some of the patterns from the Day 3 lesson. With students, brainstorm a list of words using these rime patterns. This can be done in several different ways:

- The whole group brainstorms with you and makes a list.
- Assign the same or different patterns to partners or small groups. Have them create a list of words to share with the class.
- Make the small-group assignment competitive. Choose a pattern and let each group take turns adding a word to the list until only one group is able to add a word. You might want to let groups use a dictionary to verify their words.

Day 5: Word Smart

Distribute the Lesson 25 words and ask students to arrange them across the top of their desk with plenty of workspace below. Have students respond to your questions by picking up the correct word card(s) and holding it so you can see their answer. If there are more than two correct answers, tell students to show only two—one in each hand. Ask students, "Can you find the . . ."

- word that rhymes with bind?
- word that rhymes with hoarse?
- word that is hiding something that starts a car?
- word that rhymes with a place where you live?
- word hiding the taste of a lemon?
- word that is a compound?
- word that could be prey to a hawk or cat?
- word that makes an /f/ sound but has no f?
- word hiding something straight that is made of wood?
- word with a prefix that means "between"?
- word that, if you added it to a grown boy, would mean "people all over the world"?
- word that means "a place where information is located"?
- word that is a resource for finding lots of information?
- word with 1 syllable? 4 syllables?
- word that fits in this sentence: "Let me check the citation to be sure the information is _____."?

❋ Homework ❋

After Day 5, words go home with students. They review the words and use them to complete the Parent-Child Word Work page (see page 128).

Day 1: Meet the Words

Have students pull apart the 8 word cards for this lesson and arrange the cards across the top of their desk. Then ask them to do the following:

- Hold up each card as you pronounce the word on it.
- Look at the word, read it aloud, and spell it with you.
- Return the word card to the top of their desk.

Say each word. Provide a simple definition as necessary and share some of its features as described below. You may want to have students use their fingers to cover certain letters to isolate phonic elements such as initial letters, blends, vowels, or hidden words, or point to certain letters as you discuss them. Clap the syllables in each word, and use it in a sentence that helps students understand the meaning of the word.

Some notable features of these words include the following:

* **carry**: frequently-used word; *-arry* spelling pattern helps spell words such as *marry, tarry, Harry, Barry*; double consonant; 2 syllables; hidden word: *car*

* **small**: frequently-used word; *s*-blend: *sm*; *-all* spelling pattern helps spell words such as *tall, mall, ball*; double consonant; hidden words: *ma, mall, all*

* **table**: academic word for a chart of numbers arranged in columns and rows to show facts; multiple meaning can also be a piece of furniture that provides a surface for serving food; /l/ sound is tricky and can be made a number of ways in different words: *al, el, le*; long-*a* sound; 2 syllables; hidden words: *tab, able*

* **possessive**: word used often in language arts for words to show ownership (Hannah's book, his turn, their home, parents' meeting); tricky spelling—must remember double s twice: *oss, ess*; *-ive* suffix changes verb *possess* into an adjective; 3 syllables, hidden word: *possess*

* **area**: word used often in math to mean "the surface space measured in square units"; example activity: students trace their handprints and shade the area inside the lines; 3 syllables for this small word; hidden word: *are*

* **perimeter**: word used often in math to mean "the distance around a two-dimensional space"; example activity: have students use the handprint shaded for area and trace its outline with a color to show the perimeter; 4 syllables; word part *peri* means "around"; word part *meter* means "measure"; hidden words: *me, met, meter, rim*

* **capacity**: word used often in math to mean "how much something can hold"; example activity: show capacity of 1 gallon of water, which equals 4 quarts or 8 cups; also means

"the ability to hold or contain," as in "The capacity of the auditorium is 400 students."; 4 syllables; hidden words: *cap, city, it*

* **elapsed**: word used frequently in math related to time that has passed, as in "If we got to school at 8 a.m. and it's now 10:30 a.m., 2½ hours have elapsed."; 2 syllables; hidden words: *lap, lapse*

Day 2: Word Whittle

Distribute the plastic bags containing this week's words or ask students to retrieve them. Have students place the words across the top of their workspace. After you read the first clue, they pull down all the words that fit it. For each subsequent clue in the set, students continue to whittle the words by returning those that don't fit to the top of their workspace. No new words can be added to the group after the first clue. Only one word will remain after the final clue in a set. Students return the word card to the top of their workspace before the next set of clues begins.

First Set:
1. a word that has double consonants (*carry, small, possessive*)
2. a word that has a letter that goes below the line (*carry, possessive*)
3. a word that has more than 1 syllable (*carry, possessive*)
4. a word that has 2 double consonants (*possessive*)

Second Set:
1. a word that has more than 1 syllable (*carry, table, possessive, area, perimeter, capacity, elapsed*)
2. a word that has more than 2 syllables (*possessive, area, perimeter, capacity*)
3. a word that starts with a consonant (*possessive, perimeter, capacity*)
4. a word that means "the outside border of an area" (*perimeter*)

Third Set:
1. a word that has an *a* (*small, table, area, capacity, elapsed*)
2. a word that has 2 *a*'s (*area, capacity*)
3. a word that has no tall letters or letters that go below the line (*area*)

Fourth Set:
1. a word that has fewer than 6 letters (*carry, small, table, area*)
2. a word that has more than 1 syllable (*carry, table, area*)
3. a word that ends with a vowel (*table, area*)
4. a word that ends with the same sound as *travel* (*table*)

Stump the Class

Give pairs or small groups time to work together to find relationships among this week's words. Once they have found a category into which several of the words fit, they should write the

words in a circle on the Word Clusters sheet (see page 127) and the category underneath. Allow time for each pair or group to share one set of their words and ask the rest of the class to guess the category. Even though the other students may suggest a legitimate category, only the presenters' category is the correct answer. The goal is to stump the rest of the class with a unique category. (You might discover categories that you can add to the Day 5: Word Smart activity.)

Day 3: Word Builder

Have students separate the letters at the bottom of this week's word template. Ask them to spell words as you call them out. Have students construct words based on patterns in the words and call out words in increasingly difficult order as shown below. The final word should answer this clue: These are small animals that make good pets. (*guinea pigs*)

age	sip	gain	nag	peg
page	snip	pain	sag	egg
paging	nap	pains	gag	eggs
aging	snap	sing	gang	use
pig	pug	singing	sang	using
pigs	pugs			guinea pigs
piggies				

As students spell each word, write it on the board. Ask them to cross-check their spelling with yours and correct any errors. On the board or in a pocket chart, sort the words according to the following spelling patterns:

-age	-ip	-ap	-ain	-ag	-ang
age	sip	nap	gain	nag	gang
page	snip	snap	pain	sag	sang
				gag	

After all the words have been spelled and sorted, have students read over the list, emphasizing the spelling pattern from the first vowel to the end of each word. In the case of multisyllabic words, the rimes are a bit different, so stress the rhymes of these words.

Tell students that these patterns can help them spell many other words. The Day 4 activity will start with these patterns.

Take an opportunity to talk about the following elements: word ending changes (*age/aging, page/paging, pig/pigs/piggies, pug/pugs, pain/pains, sing/singing, egg/eggs, use/using*).

Day 4: Rhymer

Return to some of the patterns from the Day 3 lesson. With students, brainstorm a list of words using these rime patterns. This can be done in several different ways:

- The whole group brainstorms with you and makes a list.
- Assign the same or different patterns to partners or small groups. Have them create a list of words to share with the class.
- Make the small-group assignment competitive. Choose a pattern and let each group take turns adding a word to the list until only one group is able to add a word. You might want to let groups use a dictionary to verify their words.

Day 5: Word Smart

Distribute the Lesson 26 words and ask students to arrange them across the top of their desk with plenty of workspace below. Have students respond to your questions by picking up the correct word card(s) and holding it so you can see their answer. If there are more than two correct answers, tell students to show only two—one in each hand. Ask students, "Can you find the . . ."

- word that means the opposite of *large*?
- word that refers to surface space?
- word hiding an automobile?
- word that names something you can eat at?
- word that means "a chart of numbers arranged in rows and columns"?
- word that tells you something is owned?
- word that is the longest in this lesson? the shortest?
- word with 4 syllables?
- word hiding a large town?
- word hiding a place on which a baby might sit?
- word that is the border of an area?
- word that lets you know that time has passed?
- word with a word part that means "measure"?
- word that rhymes with *fall*?
- word that is a verb?
- word that fits in this sentence: "The _____ of the pitcher is 1 gallon."?
- words hiding a mother and father?
- word that has 4 *s*'s?
- word that starts like the word *smart*?

Day 1: Meet the Words

Have students pull apart the 8 word cards for this lesson and arrange the cards across the top of their desk. Then ask them to do the following:

- Hold up each card as you pronounce the word on it.
- Look at the word, read it aloud, and spell it with you.
- Return the word card to the top of their desk.

Say each word. Provide a simple definition as necessary and share some of its features as described below. You may want to have students use their fingers to cover certain letters to isolate phonic elements such as initial letters, blends, vowels, or hidden words, or point to certain letters as you discuss them. Clap the syllables in each word, and use it in a sentence that helps students understand the meaning of the word.

Some notable features of these words include the following:

* **show**: frequently-used word; -ow spelling pattern helps spell words such as *grow, know, blow, flow*; hidden word: *how*

* **whether**: frequently-used word; /wh/ beginning; often confused with *weather*; 2 syllables; hidden words: *he, her, the*

* **weather**: word used often in science; refers to the atmospheric conditions—temperature, wind, cloudiness, pressure; /w/ beginning; be careful to distinguish from *whether*; 2 syllables; hidden words: *eat, we, her, the, he*

* **threaten**: word used often in science when it refers to weather conditions that present danger, as in "The hurricane will threaten the East Coast."; common use of word also (*verb*) "to endanger," as in "His father threatened to take away TV if his grades didn't improve."; consonant cluster *thr-* at beginning, like *throw, thrift, through*; 2 syllables; hidden words: *eat, at, eaten, ten*

* **thrive**: word used often in science and social studies referring to plants, environments, region, or groups of people that grow, flourish, and/or develop; /thr/ beginning sound, as in *threaten, throw*; long-*i* sound; -ive spelling pattern helps spell words such as *hive, live*

* **thermometer**: word used often in science to refer to an instrument that measures temperature; word part *therm* means "heat"; word part *meter* means "measure"; 4 syllables; hidden words: *the, meter, me, mom, met*

* **discuss**: academic word used in all content areas; means "to talk or write about," as in "We will discuss this chapter as soon as we finish reading it."; 2 syllables; hidden words: *cuss, is*

* **beautiful**: frequently-used word; synonyms are *lovely, pretty, handsome*; base word *beauty*; 3 syllables; hidden words: *be, beau, if*

Day 2: Word Whittle

Distribute the plastic bags containing this week's words or ask students to retrieve them. Have students place the words across the top of their workspace. After you read the first clue, they pull down all the words that fit it. For each subsequent clue in the set, students continue to whittle the words by returning those that don't fit to the top of their workspace. No new words can be added to the group after the first clue. Only one word will remain after the final clue in a set. Students return the word card to the top of their workspace before the next set of clues begins.

First Set:

1. a word that starts with 2 or more consonants (*show, whether, threaten, thrive, thermometer*)
2. a word that starts with *th* (*threaten, thrive, thermometer*)
3. a word that starts with *thr* (*threaten, thrive*)
4. a word that means "to grow and develop" (*thrive*)

Second Set:

1. a word that has an *e* as one of its last 2 letters (*whether, weather, threaten, thrive, thermometer*)
2. a word that has 3 tall letters (*whether, threaten, thermometer*)
3. a word that has 2 syllables (*whether, threaten*)
4. a word that starts the same way *where* starts (*whether*)

Third Set:

1. a word that has 2 syllables (*whether, weather, threaten, discuss*)
2. a word that ends with -er (*whether, weather*)
3. a word that has *th* in the middle (*whether, weather*)
4. a word that refers to the conditions in the atmosphere (*weather*)

Fourth Set:

1. a word that has at least 2 tall letters (*whether, weather, threaten, thrive, thermometer, beautiful*)
2. a word that has at least 3 tall letters (*whether, threaten, thermometer, beautiful*)
3. a word that has an *a* (*threaten, beautiful*)
4. a word that has a suffix that means "full of" (*beautiful*)

Stump the Class

Give pairs or small groups time to work together to find relationships among this week's words. Once they have found a category into which several of the words fit, they should write the words in a circle on the Word Clusters sheet (see page 127) and the category underneath. Allow time for each pair or group to share one set of their words and ask the rest of the class to guess the category. Even though the other students may suggest a legitimate

category, only the presenters' category is the correct answer. The goal is to stump the rest of the class with a unique category. (You might discover categories that you can add to the Day 5: Word Smart activity.)

Day 3: Word Builder

Have students separate the letters at the bottom of this week's word template. Ask them to spell words as you call them out. Have students construct words based on patterns in the words and call out words in increasingly difficult order as shown below. The final word should answer this clue: This weather will threaten many people. (*hurricanes*)

ash	ace	air	each	ear	sane
cash	race	hair	reach	hear	cane
crash	chase	chair	care	rear	canes
rush	chaser	rich	share	sear	hurricanes
crush		richer	ranch		
		riches	ranches		

As students spell each word, write it on the board. Ask them to cross-check their spelling with yours and correct any errors. On the board or in a pocket chart, sort the words according to the following spelling patterns:

-ash	-ush	-ace	-air	-each	-ear	-ane
ash	rush	ace	air	each	ear	sane
cash	crush	race	hair	reach	hear	cane
crash			chair		rear	
					sear	

After all the words have been spelled and sorted, have students read over the list, emphasizing the spelling pattern from the first vowel to the end of each word. In the case of multisyllabic words, the rimes are a bit different, so stress the rhymes of these words.

Tell students that these patterns can help them spell many other words. The Day 4 activity will start with these patterns.

Take an opportunity to talk about the following element: word endings (*chase/chaser, ranch/ranches, cane/canes*).

Day 4: Rhymer

Return to some of the patterns from the Day 3 lesson. With students, brainstorm a list of words using these rime patterns. This can be done in several different ways:

- The whole group brainstorms with you and makes a list.
- Assign the same or different patterns to partners or small groups. Have them create a list of words to share with the class.

- Make the small-group assignment competitive. Choose a pattern and let each group take turns adding a word to the list until only one group is able to add a word. You might want to let groups use a dictionary to verify their words.

Day 5: Word Smart

Distribute the Lesson 27 words and ask students to arrange them across the top of their desk with plenty of workspace below. Have students respond to your questions by picking up the correct word card(s) and holding it so you can see their answer. If there are more than two correct answers, tell students to show only two—one in each hand. Ask students, "Can you find the . . ."

- word that rhymes with *blow*?
- word that is a synonym for *lovely*?
- word that rhymes with *alive*?
- word that names a kind of instrument?
- word that means "to talk about"?
- word hiding what you have done to your food at the end of the meal?
- word with 4 syllables?
- word hiding a question word?
- word that has a word part that means "measure"?
- word hiding a word that means "to use bad words"?
- word that has a male and a female pronoun?
- word with a word part that means "heat"?
- word that rhymes with *beehive*?
- word that ends in the *-er* sound?
- word hiding a word for what we do with food?
- word that starts the same as the word *shower*?
- word hiding an abbreviation for *mother*?
- word hiding a pronoun that stands for "several of us"?
- word that fits in this sentence: "Do you know _____ or not we have practice today."?

✳ Homework ✳

After Day 5, words go home with students. They review the words and use them to complete the Parent-Child Word Work page (see page 128).

Day 1: Meet the Words

Have students pull apart the 8 word cards for this lesson and arrange the cards across the top of their desk. Then ask them to do the following:

- Hold up each card as you pronounce the word on it.
- Look at the word, read it aloud, and spell it with you.
- Return the word card to the top of their desk.

Say each word. Provide a simple definition as necessary and share some of its features as described below. You may want to have students use their fingers to cover certain letters to isolate phonic elements such as initial letters, blends, vowels, or hidden words, or point to certain letters as you discuss them. Clap the syllables in each word, and use it in a sentence that helps students understand the meaning of the word.

Some notable features of these words include the following:

✳ **far**: frequently-used word; -ar spelling pattern helps spell words such as *jar, crowbar, tar, star, guitar*

✳ **strange**: frequently-used word; -ange spelling pattern helps spell words such as *change, arrange, range, exchange*; /str/ blend; hidden words: *ran, range, rang, an*

✳ **cause**: word used in many content areas, especially in language arts; means "the reason something else happens," as in "The rain was the cause of our picnic's being cancelled."; /au/ sound might be tricky; silent-e ending; hidden words: *use, us*

✳ **effect**: word used in many content areas, especially in language arts; means "the result of some event or action"; usually matched with cause–the effect is the result of the cause ("The rain cancelled our picnic." The rain was the cause; the cancellation of the picnic was the effect.)

✳ **hemisphere**: word used often in social studies; means "half of the globe or world"; half of globe referred to as northern and southern hemispheres or eastern and western hemispheres; word part *hemi* means "half"; word part *sphere* means "globe"; 3 syllables; hidden words: *he, hem, is, here, sphere, her*

✳ **geography**: word used often in social studies; multiple meanings: 1) the study of the science of the earth's surface or 2) the features of a region; word part *geo* means "earth"; word part *graph* means "written" (*autograph, biography, seismograph*); 4 syllables; *ph* makes *f* sound; ending *y* makes long-e sound; hidden words: *rap, graph*

✳ **landforms**: word used often in social studies; means "a feature of the earth's surface," such as mountains, coast, plains, desert; compound word; 2 syllables; plural with -s; hidden words: *land, and, an, for, form, forms, or*

✳ **arid**: word used often in social studies with study of geography and climate; adjective that describes an area without moisture, such as a desert; 2 syllables; hidden word: *rid*

Day 2: Word Whittle

Distribute the plastic bags containing this week's words or ask students to retrieve them. Have students place the words across the top of their workspace. After you read the first clue, they pull down all the words that fit it. For each subsequent clue in the set, students continue to whittle the words by returning those that don't fit to the top of their workspace. No new words can be added to the group after the first clue. Only one word will remain after the final clue in a set. Students return the word card to the top of their workspace before the next set of clues begins.

First Set:
1. a word that starts with a consonant (*far, strange, cause, hemisphere, geography, landforms*)
2. a word that ends with a vowel (*strange, cause, hemisphere*)
3. a word that has 1 syllable (*strange, cause*)
4. a word that starts in the same way *strong* does (*strange*)

Second Set:
1. a word that has more than 1 syllable (*effect, hemisphere, geography, landforms, arid*)
2. a word that starts with a vowel (*effect, arid*)
3. a word that ends with a consonant (*effect, arid*)
4. a word that has a double consonant (*effect*)

Third Set:
1. a word that ends with a silent *e* (*strange, cause, hemisphere*)
2. a word that has more than 1 vowel (*strange, cause, hemisphere*)
3. a word that has more than 2 vowels (*cause, hemisphere*)
4. a word that has more than 3 vowels (*hemisphere*)

Fourth Set:
1. a word that has 1 syllable (*far, strange, cause*)
2. a word that has an *a* (*far, strange, cause*)
3. a word that has no letters that go below the line (*far, cause*)
4. a word that rhymes with *guitar* (*far*)

Stump the Class

Give pairs or small groups time to work together to find relationships among this week's words. Once they have found a category into which several of the words fit, they should write the words in a circle on the Word Clusters sheet (see page 127) and the category underneath. Allow time for each pair or group to share one set of their words and ask the rest of the class to guess the category. Even though the other students may suggest a legitimate category, only the presenters' category is the correct answer. The goal is to stump the rest of the class with a unique category. (You might discover categories that you can add to the Day 5: Word Smart activity.)

Day 3: Word Builder

Have students separate the letters at the bottom of this week's word template. Ask them to spell words as you call them out. Have students construct words based on patterns in the words and call out words in increasingly difficult order as shown below. The final word should answer this clue: These people study landforms. (*geologists*)

toss	oil	list	log
loss	toil	gist	logs
gloss	soil	got	geologists
lose	tool	lot	
lost	stool		
less	go		
	goes		

As students spell each word, write it on the board. Ask them to cross-check their spelling with yours and correct any errors. On the board or in a pocket chart, sort the words according to the following spelling patterns:

-oss	-oil	-ool	-ist	-ot
toss	oil	tool	list	got
loss	toil	stool	gist	lot
gloss	soil			

After all the words have been spelled and sorted, have students read over the list, emphasizing the spelling pattern from the first vowel to the end of each word. In the case of multisyllabic words, the rimes are a bit different, so stress the rhymes of these words.

Tell students that these patterns can help them spell many other words. The Day 4 activity will start with these patterns.

Take an opportunity to talk about some of the following elements: geologists study the earth's surface—dirt, rocks, landforms; *geo* means "earth/soil"; *ologist* means "one who studies"; verb tenses *go/got/goes*.

Day 4: Rhymer

Return to some of the patterns from the Day 3 lesson. With students, brainstorm a list of words using these rime patterns. This can be done in several different ways:

- The whole group brainstorms with you and makes a list.
- Assign the same or different patterns to partners or small

groups. Have them create a list of words to share with the class.
- Make the small-group assignment competitive. Choose a pattern and let each group take turns adding a word to the list until only one group is able to add a word. You might want to let groups use a dictionary to verify their words.

Day 5: Word Smart

Distribute the Lesson 28 words and ask students to arrange them across the top of their desk with plenty of workspace below. Have students respond to your questions by picking up the correct word card(s) and holding it so you can see their answer. If there are more than two correct answers, tell students to show only two— one in each hand. Ask students, "Can you find the . . ."

- word that rhymes with *exchange*?
- word with a word part that means "half"?
- word hiding the name of a type of music?
- word related to the desert?
- word that is a synonym of *odd* or *unusual*?
- word with a word part that means "earth"?
- word hiding a word that means "moved faster than a walk"?
- word that makes something happen?
- word that means "result"?
- word with a word part that means "globe"?
- word that rhymes with *applause*?
- word that is the longest in this lesson? the shortest?
- word that has 4 syllables? 2 syllables?
- word hiding pronouns for boys and girls?
- word with a word part that means "write"?

Now have students isolate the words *cause* and *effect*. Write the sentences below on the board, underlining as shown. Ask students to identify the underlined part as a cause or an effect by showing the right word.

- The weather is colder and dryer, <u>so the leaves are turning colors</u>.
- <u>Ronda skipped lunch</u> and is now hungry.
- <u>She studied hard</u> and did well on her test.
- Tom earned money and <u>was able to buy a new bike</u>.

✷ Homework ✷

After Day 5, words go home with students. They review the words and use them to complete the Parent-Child Word Work page (see page 128).

Day 1: Meet the Words

Have students pull apart the 8 word cards for this lesson and arrange the cards across the top of their desk. Then ask them to do the following:

- Hold up each card as you pronounce the word on it.
- Look at the word, read it aloud, and spell it with you.
- Return the word card to the top of their desk.

Say each word. Provide a simple definition as necessary and share some of its features as described below. You may want to have students use their fingers to cover certain letters to isolate phonic elements such as initial letters, blends, vowels, or hidden words, or point to certain letters as you discuss them. Clap the syllables in each word, and use it in a sentence that helps students understand the meaning of the word.

Some notable features of these words include the following:

✳ **draw**: frequently-used word; multiple meanings: 1) "to make something using pencils or paint" or 2) "to pick something"; -aw spelling pattern helps spell words such as *claw, paw, handsaw, jaw*; hidden word: *raw*

✳ **clean**: frequently-used word; -ean spelling pattern helps spell words such as *lean, mean, bean, houseclean*; *l*-blend (*cl*) at beginning; *ea* makes long-*e* sound; hidden words: *lean, an*

✳ **round**: frequently-used word; in math, "to replace a number with the nearest multiple of 10"; -ound spelling pattern helps spell words such as *sound, mound, ground*

✳ **conclusion**: academic word used in many content areas; means "a decision reached by using clues rather than explicit information" ("Rebecca checked the food bowl, but Tyler had not eaten anything. She reached for his leash and ran out the door calling his name and whistling loudly." We might conclude that Tyler is a dog based on the clues and our inferences); remember the "clu" syllable that tells us what we must use to make meaning; 3 syllables; word part *con* means "together" or "with"; base word *conclude* (*verb*); -*sion* suffix turns the verb into a noun; hidden words: *con, on, us*

✳ **details**: academic word used in many content areas; applied to reading and writing; means "the facts or specific information that supports the main idea"; 2 syllables; plural with -*s* ending; hidden words: *tail, tails, ail*

✳ **decimal**: word used often in math; a number that contains a ten-based fraction, such as 3.15; word part *dec* means "ten," as in *decade* (10 years); *deci* means "one-tenth"; 3 syllables; hidden words: *Dec* as abbreviation of December, *ma*

✳ **equivalent**: word used often in math; means "has the same value as," as in equivalent fractions (1/2 = 2/4); word part *equi-* means "equal"; 4 syllables

✳ **estimate**: word used often in math; (*verb*) means "to figure or calculate an answer based on judgment"; (*noun*) "an answer based on an informed guess, not accuracy"; 3 syllables; hidden words: *ma, mate, ate, at*

Day 2: Word Whittle

Distribute the plastic bags containing this week's words or ask students to retrieve them. Have students place the words across the top of their workspace. After you read the first clue, they pull down all the words that fit it. For each subsequent clue in the set, students continue to whittle the words by returning those that don't fit to the top of their workspace. No new words can be added to the group after the first clue. Only one word will remain after the final clue in a set. Students return the word card to the top of their workspace before the next set of clues begins.

First Set:

1. a word that has an *i* (*conclusion, details, decimal, equivalent, estimate*)
2. a word that has 3 syllables (*conclusion, decimal, estimate*)
3. a word that has 2 tall letters (*decimal, estimate*)
4. a word that shows tenths, hundredths, and so on (*decimal*)

Second Set:

1. a word that starts with a letter that comes before *f* in the alphabet (*draw, clean, conclusion, details, decimal, equivalent, estimate*)
2. a word that starts with a *d* (*draw, details, decimal*)
3. a word that starts with *de* (*details, decimal*)
4. a word that means "facts that support a main idea" (*details*)

Third Set:

1. a word that has a *c* and an *l* (*clean, conclusion, decimal*)
2. a word that has only 1 tall letter (*clean, conclusion*)
3. a word that ends with an *n* (*clean, conclusion*)
4. a word that means "result or end" (*conclusion*)

Fourth Set:

1. a word that has 1 syllable (*draw, clean, round*)
2. a word that has 1 tall letter (*draw, clean, round*)
3. a word that starts with a consonant blend (*draw, clean*)
4. a word that rhymes with *paw* (*draw*)

Stump the Class

Give pairs or small groups time to work together to find relationships among this week's words. Once they have found a

category into which several of the words fit, they should write the words in a circle on the Word Clusters sheet (see page 127) and the category underneath. Allow time for each pair or group to share one set of their words and ask the rest of the class to guess the category. Even though the other students may suggest a legitimate category, only the presenters' category is the correct answer. The goal is to stump the rest of the class with a unique category. (You might discover categories that you can add to the Day 5: Word Smart activity.)

Day 3: Word Builder

Have students separate the letters at the bottom of this week's word template. Ask them to spell words as you call them out. Have students construct words based on patterns in the words and call out words in increasingly difficult order as shown below. The final word should answer this clue: Rounding will help when you are doing this. (*estimating*)

team	time	eat	sing	net
steam	timing	eating	sting	magnet
steaming	gate	meat	age	ignite
game	mate	seat	sage	estimating
same	state	ant	stage	
	taste	giant	image	
	tasting			

As students spell each word, write it on the board. Ask them to cross-check their spelling with yours and correct any errors. On the board or in a pocket chart, sort the words according to the following spelling patterns:

-ame	-ate	-eat	-ing	-age	-net
game	gate	eat	sing	age	magnet
same	mate	meat	sting	sage	
	state	seat		stage	
				image	

After all the words have been spelled and sorted, have students read over the list, emphasizing the spelling pattern from the first vowel to the end of each word. In the case of multisyllabic words, the rimes are a bit different, so stress the rhymes of these words.

Tell students that these patterns can help them spell many other words. The Day 4 activity will start with these patterns.

Take an opportunity to talk about the following element: *-ing* endings (*time/timing, steam/steaming, eat/eating.*)

Day 4: Rhymer

Return to some of the patterns from the Day 3 lesson. With students, brainstorm a list of words using these rime patterns. This can be done in several different ways:

- The whole group brainstorms with you and makes a list.
- Assign the same or different patterns to partners or small groups. Have them create a list of words to share with the class.
- Make the small-group assignment competitive. Choose a pattern and let each group take turns adding a word to the list until only one group is able to add a word. You might want to let groups use a dictionary to verify their words.

Day 5: Word Smart

Distribute the Lesson 29 words and ask students to arrange them across the top of their desk with plenty of workspace below. Have students respond to your questions by picking up the correct word card(s) and holding it so you can see their answer. If there are more than two correct answers, tell students to show only two—one in each hand. Ask students, "Can you find the . . ."

- word that rhymes with *sound*? *mean*?
- word that starts the same way *convention* starts?
- word that has 5 letters?
- word hiding the opposite of *fat*? the ends of animals?
- word that fits in this sentence: "One-half and three-sixths are _____ fractions."?
- word that is the longest in this lesson? the shortest?
- word that has a word part that means "equal"?
- word hiding something that hasn't been cooked?
- word with a word part that means "tenth"?
- word that means "a decision based on a person's best judgment"?
- word that means "an end or answer based on clues"?
- word that supports a big picture idea?
- word whose synonym may be *illustrate* or *pick*?
- word that describes a shape?
- word that is plural?
- word hiding something you did to your meal yesterday?
- word that fits in this sentence: "Can you _____ how many pieces of candy are in the jar."?

❋ Homework ❋

After Day 5, words go home with students. They review the words and use them to complete the Parent-Child Word Work page (see page 128).

Day 1: Meet the Words

Have students pull apart the 8 word cards for this lesson and arrange the cards across the top of their desk. Then ask them to do the following:

- Hold up each card as you pronounce the word on it.
- Look at the word, read it aloud, and spell it with you.
- Return the word card to the top of their desk.

Say each word. Provide a simple definition as necessary and share some of its features as described below. You may want to have students use their fingers to cover certain letters to isolate phonic elements such as initial letters, blends, vowels, or hidden words, or point to certain letters as you discuss them. Clap the syllables in each word, and use it in a sentence that helps students understand the meaning of the word.

Some notable features of these words include the following:

✳ **grow**: frequently-used word; -ow pattern helps spell other words such as *blow, grow, low, throw*; hidden word: *row*

✳ **together**: frequently-used word; adverb; 3 syllables; hidden words: *to, get, her, he, the*

✳ **thought**: frequently-used word; /th/ sound at beginning; *gh* is silent; *ou* makes /aw/ sound; -ought spelling pattern helps spell words such as *bought, sought, fought, ought*; hidden word: *ought*

✳ **between**: frequently-used word; preposition like *over, under, in, out*; 2 syllables; hidden words: *be, bet, tween* (slang), *wee*

✳ **sentence**: academic word frequently used in language arts; a complete sentence 1) expresses a complete thought, 2) has end punctuation, 3) starts with a capital letter; 2 syllables; hidden word: *ten, sent*

✳ **summarize**: academic word used in all content areas; means "to give a brief outline of what has been read, heard, or written"; 3 syllables; hidden words: *sum, ma, mar*

✳ **example**: academic word used in all content areas; a sample that shows the character of the whole; 3 syllables; hidden words: *am, amp, ample, exam*

✳ **answer**: academic word used in all content areas; means "a response to a question"; the *w* is silent and tricky for spelling; 2 syllables; hidden word: *an*

Day 2: Word Whittle

Distribute the plastic bags containing this week's words or ask students to retrieve them. Have students place the words across the top of their workspace. After you read the first clue, they pull down all the words that fit it. For each subsequent clue in the set, students continue to whittle the words by returning those that don't fit to the top of their workspace. No new words can be added to the group after the first clue. Only one word will remain after the final clue in a set. Students return the word card to the top of their workspace before the next set of clues begins.

First Set:

1. a word that has 3 syllables (*together, summarize, example*)
2. a word that has at least 3 vowels (*together, summarize, example*)
3. a word that has a silent e at the end (*summarize, example*)
4. a word that means "to give a brief outline of what has been read, written, or heard" (*summarize*)

Second Set:

1. a word that has no more than 2 syllables (*grow, thought, between, sentence, answer*)
2. a word with a tall letter (*thought, between, sentence*)
3. a word with a *t* (*thought, between, sentence*)
4. a word that begins and ends with the same letter (*thought*)

Third Set:

1. a word that ends with a consonant (*grow, together, thought, between, answer*)
2. a word that has a *g* (*grow, together, thought*)
3. a word that has a /th/ sound (*together, thought*)
4. a word that has a pronoun hiding (*together*)

Fourth Set:

1. a word that has a consonant as its second letter (*grow, thought, example, answer*)
2. a word that has a silent letter (*thought, example, answer*)
3. a word that starts with a vowel (*example, answer*)
4. a word that has 3 syllables (*example*)

Stump the Class

Give pairs or small groups time to work together to find relationships among this week's words. Once they have found a category into which several of the words fit, they should write the words in a circle on the Word Clusters sheet (see page 127) and the category underneath. Allow time for each pair or group to share one set of their words and ask the rest of the class to guess the category. Even though the other students may suggest a legitimate

category, only the presenters' category is the correct answer. The goal is to stump the rest of the class with a unique category. (You might discover categories that you can add to the Day 5: Word Smart activity.)

Day 3: Word Builder

Have students separate the letters at the bottom of this week's word template. Ask them to spell words as you call them out. Have students construct words based on patterns in the words and call out words in increasingly difficult order as shown below. The final word should answer this clue: These are answers. (*solutions*)

it	out	into	list	slot
sit	snout	onto	lists	slots
lit	oil	tool	lot	tonsils
unit	soil	stool	lots	solutions
	toil			

As students spell each word, write it on the board. Ask them to cross-check their spelling with yours and correct any errors. On the board or in a pocket chart, sort the words according to the following spelling patterns:

-it	-out	-oil	-ool	-ot
it	out	oil	tool	lot
sit	snout	soil	stool	slot
lit		toil		
unit				

After all the words have been spelled and sorted, have students read over the list, emphasizing the spelling pattern from the first vowel to the end of each word. In the case of multisyllabic words, the rimes are a bit different, so stress the rhymes of these words.

Tell students that these patterns can help them spell many other words. The Day 4 activity will start with these patterns.

Take an opportunity to talk about some of the following elements: -s endings, s-blends: *sl, sn, st.*

Day 4: Rhymer

Return to some of the patterns from the Day 3 lesson. With students, brainstorm a list of words using these rime patterns. This can be done in several different ways:

- The whole group brainstorms with you and makes a list.
- Assign the same or different patterns to partners or small groups. Have them create a list of words to share with the class.
- Make the small-group assignment competitive. Choose a pattern and let each group take turns adding a word to the list until only one group is able to add a word. You might want to let groups use a dictionary to verify their words.

Day 5: Word Smart

Distribute the Lesson 30 words and ask students to arrange them across the top of their desk with plenty of workspace below. Have students respond to your questions by picking up the correct word card(s) and holding it so you can see their answer. If there are more than two correct answers, tell students to show only two—one in each hand. Ask students, "Can you find the . . ."

- word that rhymes with *slow*?
- word hiding something that corn grows in?
- word that is the opposite of a question?
- word hiding a math term for what you get when you add numbers together?
- word that rhymes with *bought*?
- word that has 3 syllables?
- word that has 1 syllable?
- word that begins and ends with the same letter?
- word that is how we want to work in our classroom?
- word that fits in this sentence: "It is good to see an _____ before doing all of the problems on your own."?
- word that has a silent *gh*?
- word with a long-*i* sound?
- word that rhymes with *caught*?
- word that has a number hiding in it?
- word hiding a big test?
- word that needs a capital letter and end punctuation?
- word that has a silent *w*?
- word that is a preposition?
- word that has a double consonant?
- word that is sometimes *yes* or *no*?
- word that has a /th/ sound?

Day 1: Meet the Words

Have students pull apart the 8 word cards for this lesson and arrange the cards across the top of their desk. Then ask them to do the following:

- Hold up each card as you pronounce the word on it.
- Look at the word, read it aloud, and spell it with you.
- Return the word card to the top of their desk.

Say each word. Provide a simple definition as necessary and share some of its features as described below. You may want to have students use their fingers to cover certain letters to isolate phonic elements such as initial letters, blends, vowels, or hidden words, or point to certain letters as you discuss them. Clap the syllables in each word, and use it in a sentence that helps students understand the meaning of the word.

Some notable features of these words include the following:

❋ **young**: frequently-used word; /y/ beginning sound; tricky vowel partners *ou*; /ng/ sound at end

❋ **laugh**: frequently-used word; *gh* makes /f/ sound; also tricky *au* vowel partners

❋ **family**: frequently-used word; tricky *i* is often slighted in pronunciation; show plural form *families*, removing *y* and adding *-ies*; 3 syllables; hidden word: *am*

❋ **children**: frequently-used word; /ch/ sound and *r*-blend: *dr*; plural of *child*; 2 syllables; hidden word: *hi, child*

❋ **infection**: word used often in science/health; means "having germs or disease"; prefix *in-* means "in or into"; suffix *-tion* turns *infect* into a noun—"state of being infected"; 3 syllables; hidden words: *in, on, infect*

❋ **parasite**: word used often in science; an organism that lives on another organism (the host); outside of science, this term may be used to refer to someone who survives off of someone else; *para-* means "beside"; silent-*e* ending; 3 syllables; hidden words: *pa, par, sit, site, it, as*

❋ **prescribe**: word used often in science/health, meaning "to order the use of medicine" (*done by a doctor*); prefix *pre-* means "earlier or before," as in before the illness or to prevent further illness; word part *scrib* means "to write"; tidbit: At one time in history, scribes were employed to copy documents by hand in contrast to the copy machines of today; silent *e* ending; 2 syllables; hidden words: *scribe, rib, be*

❋ **physical**: word used often in science/health; multiple meanings: 1) (*adjective*) related to the body, as in physical exercise, and 2) (*noun*) a wellness check-up given by a qualified physician; *ph* makes /f/ sound; *-al* is tricky as the sound is also spelled *-le* and *-el* in some words; word part *phys* means "body or medicine" (*physique, physician*); 3 syllables

Day 2: Word Whittle

Distribute the plastic bags containing this week's words or ask students to retrieve them. Have students place the words across the top of their workspace. After you read the first clue, they pull down all the words that fit it. For each subsequent clue in the set, students continue to whittle the words by returning those that don't fit to the top of their workspace. No new words can be added to the group after the first clue. Only one word will remain after the final clue in a set. Students return the word card to the top of their workspace before the next set of clues begins.

First Set:

1. a word that has a letter that goes below the line (*young, laugh, family, parasite, prescribe, physical*)
2. a word that has 3 syllables (*family, parasite, physical*)
3. a word that starts with a *p* (*parasite, physical*)
4. a word that starts with an /f/ sound (*physical*)

Second Set:

1. a word that starts with a *p* (*parasite, prescribe, physical*)
2. a word that ends with a silent letter (*parasite, prescribe*)
3. a word that has at least 3 vowels (*parasite, prescribe*)
4. a word that is a verb (*prescribe*)

Third Set:

1. a word that has 2 vowels together (*young, laugh, infection*)
2. a word that has 1 syllable (*young, laugh*)
3. a word that has a *g* (*young, laugh*)
4. a word that ends with the same sound as *cough* (*laugh*)

Fourth Set:

1. a word that is related to medicine (*infection, parasite, prescribe, physical*)
2. a word that has an *i* and a *c* (*infection, prescribe, physical*)
3. a word that has 3 syllables (*infection, physical*)
4. a word that names something a doctor might write a prescription for (*infection*)

Stump the Class

Give pairs or small groups time to work together to find relationships among this week's words. Once they have found a category into which several of the words fit, they should write the words in a circle on the Word Clusters sheet (see page 127) and the category underneath. Allow time for each pair or group to share one set of their words and ask the rest of the class to guess the category. Even though the other students may suggest a legitimate category, only the presenters' category is the correct answer. The goal is to stump the rest of the class with a unique category. (You might discover categories that you can add to the Day 5: Word Smart activity.)

Day 3: Word Builder

Have students separate the letters at the bottom of this week's word template. Ask them to spell words as you call them out. Have students construct words based on patterns in the words and call out words in increasingly difficult order as shown below. The final word should answer this clue: These may come in handy if you have an infection. (antibiotics)

at	attic	bias	taco
cat	act	oat	tacos
scat	action	boat	tonic
bat	actions	coat	bionic
bats	ant	scab	citation
	antics	basic	antibiotics
		bacon	

As students spell each word, write it on the board. Ask them to cross-check their spelling with yours and correct any errors. On the board or in a pocket chart, sort the words according to the following spelling patterns:

-at	-oat	-ic
at	oat	tonic
cat	boat	bionic
scat	coat	
bat		

After all the words have been spelled and sorted, have students read over the list, emphasizing the spelling pattern from the first vowel to the end of each word. In the case of multisyllabic words, the rimes are a bit different, so stress the rhymes of these words.

Tell students that these patterns can help them spell many other words. The Day 4 activity will start with these patterns.

Take an opportunity to talk about some of the following elements: bio- means "life": bionic, biography, autobiography, antibiotic (against living organisms that are harming your system); anti- means "against." Review previous word citation.

Day 4: Rhymer

Return to some of the patterns from the Day 3 lesson. With students, brainstorm a list of words using these rime patterns. This can be done in several different ways:

- The whole group brainstorms with you and makes a list.

- Assign the same or different patterns to partners or small groups. Have them create a list of words to share with the class.
- Make the small-group assignment competitive. Choose a pattern and let each group take turns adding a word to the list until only one group is able to add a word. You might want to let groups use a dictionary to verify their words.

Day 5: Word Smart

Distribute the Lesson 31 words and ask students to arrange them across the top of their desk with plenty of workspace below. Have students respond to your questions by picking up the correct word card(s) and holding it so you can see their answer. If there are more than two correct answers, tell students to show only two—one in each hand. Ask students, "Can you find the . . ."

- word that is the opposite of cry?
- word that has ancestors?
- word that has a prefix meaning "beside"?
- word that means "to order the use of medicine"?
- word that rhymes with half?
- word that rhymes with strung?
- word that means "a wellness check-up"?
- word that is the opposite of old?
- word hiding a person from long ago who made handwritten copies of documents?
- word hiding a greeting we hear every day?
- word with the same prefix as paratrooper?
- word with a prefix that means "in or into"?
- word that represents mother, grandmother, brother, sister?
- word hiding a word that means "place"?
- word with a suffix that changed it from a verb into a noun?
- word hiding its singular form?
- word that makes an /f/ sound but has no f?
- words of which one is part of the other?
- words of which one describes the other?
- words that fit in this sentence: "When he went for his _____, the doctor had to _____ some medicine."?

✳ Homework ✳

After Day 5, words go home with students. They review the words and use them to complete the Parent-Child Word Work page (see page 128).

Systematic Word Study for Grades 2–3 © 2011 by Cheryl M. Sigmon, Scholastic Teaching Resources • Lesson 31   83

Day 1: Meet the Words

Have students pull apart the 8 word cards for this lesson and arrange the cards across the top of their desk. Then ask them to do the following:

- Hold up each word as you pronounce it.
- Look at the word, read it aloud, and spell it together.
- Return the word to the top of the desk.

Single out each word and some of its features shown below. Have students cover letters with their hands and point to letters you mention. Clap syllables, and use each word in a sentence that helps students' understanding of it.

Some notable features include the following:

✳ **inside**: frequently-used word; compound word; preposition like *above, around, over, under*; 2 syllables; hidden words: *in, side*

✳ **watch**: frequently-used word; *-atch* spelling pattern helps spell other words such as *patch, batch, match*, although the rhyme is not exact; verb usage, as in "Let's watch the parade from the balcony."; also, noun usage, as in a timepiece worn on the arm; hidden word: *at*

✳ **somewhere**: frequently-used word; compound word; 2 syllables; hidden words: *so, some, me, where, he, her, here*

✳ **subset**: word used frequently in math; means that a set of numbers is part of a larger group of numbers (*best demonstrated with a quick drawing*); prefix *sub-* means "under or below," as in *submarine* ("under water") or *substitute* teacher ("under direction of regular teacher") or *subterranean* ("under the earth"); *-et* spelling pattern helps spell words such as *set, met, get, target*; 2 syllables; hidden words: *set, sub*

✳ **frequency**: word used often in math and also in general usage; means "how often something occurs"; in math, frequency refers to the number of times a number appears in a set of data; 3 syllables

✳ **integer**: word used often in math; one of the set of all positive and negative whole numbers and zero (does not include decimals and fractions); 3 syllables; hidden word: *in*

✳ **infinite**: word used often in math and also in general usage; means "endless"; prefix *in-* means "not"; 3 syllables; hidden words: *in, finite, it*

✳ **coordinates**: word used often in math; means "a set of numbers that describes the location of a point on a plane"; 4 syllables; plural; prefix *co-* means "with or together"; hidden words: *or, in, at, ate*

Day 2: Word Whittle

Distribute the plastic bags containing this week's words or ask students to retrieve them. Have students place the words across the top of their workspace. After you read the first clue, they pull down all the words that fit it. For each subsequent clue in the set, students continue to whittle the words by returning those that don't fit to the top of their workspace. No new words can be added to the group after the first clue. Only one word will remain after the final clue in a set. Students return the word card to the top of their workspace before the next set of clues begins.

First Set:

1. a word that has 2 syllables (*inside, somewhere, subset*)
2. a word that has tall letters (*inside, somewhere, subset*)
3. a word that is a compound (*inside, somewhere*)
4. a word that has a /hw/ sound (*somewhere*)

Second Set:

1. a word that has 3 syllables (*frequency, integer, infinite, coordinates*)
2. a word that has a *t* (*integer, infinite, coordinates*)
3. a word that refers to numbers (*integer*)

Third Set:

1. a word that has an *s* (*inside, somewhere, subset, coordinates*)
2. a word that is often used in math (*subset, coordinates*)
3. a word that has at least 2 syllables (*subset, coordinates*)
4. a word that has 4 syllables (*coordinates*)

Fourth Set:

1. a word that has at least 3 vowels (*inside, somewhere, frequency, integer, infinite, coordinates*)
2. a word that has at least 4 vowels (*somewhere, infinite, coordinates*)
3. a word that has at least 2 of the same vowel (*somewhere, infinite, coordinates*)
4. a word that has 3 of the same vowel (*infinite*)

Stump the Class

Give pairs or small groups time to work together to find relationships among this week's words. Once they have found a category into which several of the words fit, they should write the words in a circle on the Word Clusters sheet (see page 127) and the category underneath. Allow time for each pair or group to share one set of their words and ask the rest of the class to guess the category. Even though the other students may suggest a legitimate category, only the presenters' category is the correct answer. The goal is to stump the rest of the class with a unique category. (You might discover categories that you can add to the Day 5: Word Smart activity.)

Day 3: Word Builder

Have students separate the letters at the bottom of this week's word template. Ask them to spell words as you call them out. Have students construct words based on patterns in the words and call out words in increasingly difficult order as shown below. The final word should answer this clue: You'd find this below the sea. (*submarine*)

ran	bus	name	barn	near
man	busier	same	bran	smear
bear	rinse	mean	ban	marine
bare	main	bean	urban	marines
snare	rain	beam		submarine
	brain			

As students spell each word, write it on the board. Ask them to cross-check their spelling with yours and correct any errors. On the board or in a pocket chart, sort the words according to the following spelling patterns:

-an	-ain	-ean	-ear	-are
ran	main	mean	near	bare
man	rain	bean	smear	snare
bran	brain			
ban				
urban				

After all the words have been spelled and sorted, have students read over the list, emphasizing the spelling pattern from the first vowel to the end of each word. In the case of multisyllabic words, the rimes are a bit different, so stress the rhymes of these words.

Tell students that these patterns can help them spell many other words. The Day 4 activity will start with these patterns.

Take an opportunity to talk about some of the following elements: homophones (*bare/bear*), sub- means "under" (*submarine, subset, suburban*).

Day 4: Rhymer

Return to some of the patterns from the Day 3 lesson. With students, brainstorm a list of words using these rime patterns. This can be done in several different ways:

- The whole group brainstorms with you and makes a list.
- Assign the same or different patterns to partners or small groups. Have them create a list of words to share with the class.
- Make the small-group assignment competitive. Choose a pattern and let each group take turns adding a word to the list

until only one group is able to add a word. You might want to let groups use a dictionary to verify their words.

Day 5: Word Smart

Distribute the Lesson 32 words and ask students to arrange them across the top of their desk with plenty of workspace below. Have students respond to your questions by picking up the correct word card(s) and holding it so you can see their answer. If there are more than two correct answers, tell students to show only two—one in each hand. Ask students, "Can you find the . . ."

- word that has a long sandwich hiding in it?
- word that refers to something that can't be counted?
- word that is a compound?
- word that has 3 of the same vowel?
- word hiding 3 pronouns?
- word that relates to how often a number occurs in data?
- word that fits in this sentence: "Point A is located at the _____ (0, 4)."?
- word that, if you changed one letter, would be late in the day?
- word with a prefix that means "not"?
- word with 4 syllables?
- word with 3 syllables?
- word that helps you tell time?
- word that has the same prefix as a ship that travels under the sea?
- word that refers to a whole number only?
- word that is the opposite of *outside*?
- word that tells what 1 is in the sequence of numbers 1–10?
- word that can't be decimals or fractions?
- word that can be numbers of any kind?
- word that describes places?

Day 1: Meet the Words

Have students pull apart the 8 word cards for this lesson and arrange the cards across the top of their desk. Then ask them to do the following:

- Hold up each card as you pronounce the word on it.
- Look at the word, read it aloud, and spell it with you.
- Return the word card to the top of their desk.

Say each word. Provide a simple definition as necessary and share some of its features as described below. You may want to have students use their fingers to cover certain letters to isolate phonic elements such as initial letters, blends, vowels, or hidden words, or point to certain letters as you discuss them. Clap the syllables in each word, and use it in a sentence that helps students understand the meaning of the word.

Some notable features of these words include the following:

* **without**: frequently-used word; compound word; preposition; *-out* spelling patterns helps spell words such as *shout, pout, grout*; 2 syllables; hidden words: *with, it, out, wit*

* **sometimes**: frequently-used word; compound word; adverb that means "now and then" or "on some occasions"; 2 syllables; hidden words: *so, some, me, met, time, times*

* **coast**: word used often in science and social studies; describes a landform that stretches along the edge of the sea; also means "to glide"; spelling pattern *-oast* helps spell words such as *toast, roast, boast*; hidden word: *as*

* **mountains**: word used often in science and social studies; describes a landform—a natural rise in the earth's surface that has a summit or peak; plural; 2 syllables; hidden words: *mount, mountain*

* **highlands**: word used often in science and social studies; describes a landform—an elevated region; compound word; 2 syllables; hidden words: *hi, high, land, lands, and, an*

* **erosion**: word used often in science; means "the process of wearing away or destroying"; in science, often pertains to erosion of the earth by weather and other elements; 3 syllables; *-sion* suffix changes verb *erode* into a noun

* **conservation**: word used most often in science; means "the act of protecting the environment"; *-tion* suffix changes verb *conserve* into a noun; 4 syllables; hidden words: *on, con, at*

* **prairie**: word used often in science and social studies; describes a landform that is an extensive tract of land that is mostly treeless and dry, with fertile soil; tricky vowels—remember the *i*'s on either side of the *r*; 2 syllables; hidden word: *air*

Day 2: Word Whittle

Distribute the plastic bags containing this week's words or ask students to retrieve them. Have students place the words across the top of their workspace. After you read the first clue, they pull down all the words that fit it. For each subsequent clue in the set, students continue to whittle the words by returning those that don't fit to the top of their workspace. No new words can be added to the group after the first clue. Only one word will remain after the final clue in a set. Students return the word card to the top of their workspace before the next set of clues begins.

First Set:

1. a word that is a landform (*coast, mountains, highlands, prairie*)
2. a word that describes landforms that have great height (*mountains, highlands*)
3. a word that has 2 syllables (*mountains, highlands*)
4. a word that is a compound (*highlands*)

Second Set:

1. a word that is a compound (*without, sometimes, highlands*)
2. a word that has 2 syllables (*without, sometimes, highlands*)
3. a word that has an *s* (*sometimes, highlands*)
4. a word that begins and ends with the same letter (*sometimes*)

Third Set:

1. a word that has at least 1 tall letter (*without, sometimes, coast, mountains, highlands, conservation*)
2. a word that has at least 2 tall letters (*without, highlands*)
3. a word that has at least 2 vowels (*without, highlands*)
4. a word that names a landform (*highlands*)

Fourth Set:

1. a word that starts with one of the first 10 letters of the alphabet (*coast, highlands, erosion, conservation*)
2. a word that has an *o* (*coast, erosion, conservation*)
3. a word that starts with the same sound as the word *construction* (*coast, conservation*)
4. a word that describes action to protect landforms (*conservation*)

Stump the Class

Give pairs or small groups time to work together to find relationships among this week's words. Once they have found a category into which several of the words fit, they should write the words in a circle on the Word Clusters sheet (see page 127) and the category underneath. Allow time for each pair or group to share one set of their words and ask the rest of the class to guess the category. Even though the other students may suggest a legitimate category, only the presenters' category is the correct answer. The goal is to stump the rest of the class with a unique category. (You might discover categories that you can add to the Day 5: Word Smart activity.)

Day 3: Word Builder

Have students separate the letters at the bottom of this week's word template. Ask them to spell words as you call them out. Have students construct words based on patterns in the words and call out words in increasingly difficult order as shown below. The final word should answer this clue: Wind and water wore down that rock. (*weathering*)

water	hang	tear	ear	eight	earth
watering	rehang	tearing	near	weight	weather
eat	gain	white	nearing	were	weathering
heat	regain	green	night	where	
wheat			right		

As students spell each word, write it on the board. Ask them to cross-check their spelling with yours and correct any errors. On the board or in a pocket chart, sort the words according to the following spelling patterns:

-eat	-ear	-ight	-eight
eat	ear	night	eight
heat	near	right	weight
wheat			

After all the words have been spelled and sorted, have students read over the list, emphasizing the spelling pattern from the first vowel to the end of each word. In the case of multisyllabic words, the rimes are a bit different, so stress the rhymes of these words.

Tell students that these patterns can help them spell many other words. The Day 4 activity will start with these patterns.

Take an opportunity to talk about some of the following elements: endings (-*ing*), prefixes (*re*-), homophones (*tear/tear*).

Day 4: Rhymer

Return to some of the patterns from the Day 3 lesson. With students, brainstorm a list of words using these rime patterns. This can be done in several different ways:

- The whole group brainstorms with you and makes a list.
- Assign the same or different patterns to partners or small groups. Have them create a list of words to share with the class.
- Make the small-group assignment competitive. Choose a pattern and let each group take turns adding a word to the list until only one group is able to add a word. You might want to let groups use a dictionary to verify their words.

Day 5: Word Smart

Distribute the Lesson 33 words and ask students to arrange them across the top of their desk with plenty of workspace below. Have students respond to your questions by picking up the correct word card(s) and holding it so you can see their answer. If there are more than two correct answers, tell students to show only two—one in each hand. Ask students, "Can you find the . . ."

- word that is a compound?
- word that describes actions to help save landforms?
- word that means "now and then"?
- word hiding the opposite of *low*? opposite of *in*?
- word hiding what we breathe?
- word that names something that borders the ocean?
- word that names something you might climb?
- word that has 4 syllables?
- word that has 1 syllable?
- word that has a /th/ sound?
- word that is hiding a greeting?
- word that describes a whole region of elevated land?
- word that describes a large tract of mostly flat, dry, treeless land?
- words—one of which keeps the other from happening?
- word that, if you replaced the first letter with a *t*, would be something you might eat for breakfast?
- word that rhymes with *merry*?
- word that has 2 syllables?
- word hiding a pronoun?
- word that rhymes with *boast*?
- word that means the opposite of *with*?
- word that rhymes with *bands*?
- word whose suffix changes it from a verb to a noun?
- word that rhymes with *shout*?

✳ Homework ✳

After Day 5, words go home with students. They review the words and use them to complete the Parent-Child Word Work page (see page 128).

Day 1: Meet the Words

Have students pull apart the 8 word cards for this lesson and arrange the cards across the top of their desk. Then ask them to do the following:

- Hold up each card as you pronounce the word on it.
- Look at the word, read it aloud, and spell it with you.
- Return the word card to the top of their desk.

Say each word. Provide a simple definition as necessary and share some of its features as described below. You may want to have students use their fingers to cover certain letters to isolate phonic elements such as initial letters, blends, vowels, or hidden words, or point to certain letters as you discuss them. Clap the syllables in each word, and use it in a sentence that helps students understand the meaning of the word.

Some notable features of these words include the following:

* **strong**: frequently-used word; /str/ blend at beginning; *-ong* spelling pattern helps spell other words such as *wrong, belong, prong, long*; hidden word: *on*

* **other**: frequently-used word; *-other* spelling pattern helps spell other words such as *mother, brother*; usually used as an adjective; 2 syllables; hidden words: *the, he*

* **folktale**: word used often in language arts; a genre of literature whose stories share common values, thought to be passed down by generations; compound word; 2 syllables; *tale/tail* are homophones; hidden words: *folk, tale*

* **animal**: frequently-used word; tricky ending sound, as it is sometimes made by *-el* and *-le*; 3 syllables; hidden words: *an, ma*

* **eclipse**: word used often in science; a lunar eclipse occurs when the earth comes between the sun and the moon, causing a shadow to fall on the moon; a solar eclipse occurs when the moon comes between the earth and the sun, blocking out the sun's rays; 2 syllables; hidden words: *clip, clips, lip, lips*

* **gravity**: word used often in science; means "a force of nature that pulls bodies of matter together"; gravity holds our bodies to the earth; 3 syllables; hidden word: *it*

* **fossil**: word used most often in science; means "the remains, impression, or trace of a former living thing" (*plant or animal*); (*Show a picture of a fossil, if possible. Ask students what types of questions they might have about a fossil, such as "How old is it? What was it? Was it once colorful? Why did it exist? How did it live?"*); 2 syllables

* **discovery**: word used often in science and social studies; means "something found or about which knowledge is gained," such as the discovery of the New World or the discovery of a new planet; *dis-* prefix means "opposite of"; in this word–the opposite of covering up; 4 syllables; hidden words: *cover, discover, cove, very, is*

Day 2: Word Whittle

Distribute the plastic bags containing this week's words or ask students to retrieve them. Have students place the words across the top of their workspace. After you read the first clue, they pull down all the words that fit it. For each subsequent clue in the set, students continue to whittle the words by returning those that don't fit to the top of their workspace. No new words can be added to the group after the first clue. Only one word will remain after the final clue in a set. Students return the word card to the top of their workspace before the next set of clues begins.

First Set:

1. a word that has 2 syllables (*other, folktale, eclipse, fossil*)
2. a word that starts with a letter that comes before *m* in the alphabet (*folktale, eclipse, fossil*)
3. a word that starts with an /f/ sound (*folktale, fossil*)
4. a word that is a type of story (*folktale*)

Second Set:

1. a word that has at least 3 syllables (*animal, gravity, discovery*)
2. a word that has a tall letter (*animal, gravity, discovery*)
3. a word that ends with a long-e sound (*gravity, discovery*)
4. a word that means "a force of nature that pulls two bodies of matter together" (*gravity*)

Third Set:

1. a word that relates to science (*eclipse, gravity, fossil, discovery*)
2. a word that has at least 2 syllables (*eclipse, gravity, fossil, discovery*)
3. a word that begins or ends with a tall letter (*fossil, discovery*)
4. a word that is the remains from long ago of something living (*fossil*)

Fourth Set:

1. a word that has a *t* (*strong, other, folktale, gravity*)
2. a word that ends with a consonant (*strong, other, gravity*)
3. a word that begins with a consonant blend (*strong, gravity*)
4. a word that rhymes with *wrong* (*strong*)

Stump the Class

Give pairs or small groups time to work together to find relationships among this week's words. Once they have found a

category into which several of the words fit, they should write the words in a circle on the Word Clusters sheet (see page 127) and the category underneath. Allow time for each pair or group to share one set of their words and ask the rest of the class to guess the category. Even though the other students may suggest a legitimate category, only the presenters' category is the correct answer. The goal is to stump the rest of the class with a unique category. (You might discover categories that you can add to the Day 5: Word Smart activity.)

Day 3: Word Builder

Have students separate the letters at the bottom of this week's word template. Ask them to spell words as you call them out. Have students construct words based on patterns in the words and call out words in increasingly difficult order as shown below. The final word should answer this clue: There are many fossils to prove that these once roamed the earth. (*dinosaurs*)

rod	road	our	raid	air
sod	radio	ours	said	oar
nod	sound	sour	and	soar
rain	round	run	sand	dinosaurs
drain		ruin	sad	

As students spell each word, write it on the board. Ask them to cross-check their spelling with yours and correct any errors. On the board or in a pocket chart, sort the words according to the following spelling patterns:

-ain	-ound	-our	-aid	-and	-od
rain	sound	our	raid	and	rod
drain	round	sour	said	sand	sod
					nod

After all the words have been spelled and sorted, have students read over the list, emphasizing the spelling pattern from the first vowel to the end of each word. In the case of multisyllabic words, the rimes are a bit different, so stress the rhymes of these words.

Tell students that these patterns can help them spell many other words. The Day 4 activity will start with these patterns.

Take the opportunity to share this interesting fact: *raid* and *said* have the same spelling pattern but different sound patterns. The word *said* was pronounced with the same sound pattern as *raid* up until recent history.

Day 4: Rhymer

Return to some of the patterns from the Day 3 lesson. With students, brainstorm a list of words using these rime patterns. This can be done in several different ways:

- The whole group brainstorms with you and makes a list.

- Assign the same or different patterns to partners or small groups. Have them create a list of words to share with the class.
- Make the small-group assignment competitive. Choose a pattern and let each group take turns adding a word to the list until only one group is able to add a word. You might want to let groups use a dictionary to verify their words.

Day 5: Word Smart

Distribute the Lesson 34 words and ask students to arrange them across the top of their desk with plenty of workspace below. Have students respond to your questions by picking up the correct word card(s) and holding it so you can see their answer. If there are more than two correct answers, tell students to show only two—one in each hand. Ask students, "Can you find the . . ."

- word that rhymes with *mother*?
- word hiding something that might hide you?
- word naming something that might walk on 4 legs?
- word that relates to the moon and sun?
- word that has 4 syllables? 1 syllable?
- word that starts with a vowel?
- word that describes a story passed down for generations that usually teaches about values?
- word hiding a verb that means you've found something?
- word hiding a story that isn't true? something you kiss with?
- word that, if you added *br*, would be kin to you?
- word hiding another word for *people*?
- word hiding something used to hold things together?
- word that is the longest in this lesson? the shortest?
- word that ends with a silent *e*? a long-*e* sound?
- word whose *-y* ending changes it from a verb to a noun?
- word that could follow the word *solar* or *lunar*?
- word that is the opposite of *weak*?
- word that keeps us from floating off into space?
- word that gives us clues about the past?
- word with a prefix that means "the opposite of"?

Day 1: Meet the Words

Have students pull apart the 8 word cards for this lesson and arrange the cards across the top of their desk. Then ask them to do the following:

- Hold up each card as you pronounce the word on it.
- Look at the word, read it aloud, and spell it with you.
- Return the word card to the top of their desk.

Say each word. Provide a simple definition as necessary and share some of its features as described below. You may want to have students use their fingers to cover certain letters to isolate phonic elements such as initial letters, blends, vowels, or hidden words, or point to certain letters as you discuss them. Clap the syllables in each word, and use it in a sentence that helps students understand the meaning of the word.

Some notable features of these words include the following:

∗ **might**: frequently-used word; noun usage means "strength," as in *mighty*; verb usage means "maybe," as in "We might see you at the movies."; *-ight* spelling pattern helps spell words such as *fight, fright, flight, sight*; long-*i* sound; *gh* is silent

∗ **already**: frequently-used word; rhymes with *steady*; different from *all ready*: *already* means "previously" or "so soon" ("We were already planning to go by the store." "Is it time to go already?"), whereas *all ready* means "entirely ready" ("We were all ready to start field day when it began to rain."); 3 syllables; hidden words: *read, ready*

∗ **let's**: frequently-used word; easily confused with *lets*; with the apostrophe, *let's* is a contraction and can only be used when *let us* is intended, as in "Let's see if it's raining outside."; *lets* is a verb, as in "If mother lets me go, I'll be ready in an hour."; hidden word: *let*

∗ **skeleton**: word used often in science; means "the bones of an animal or human that form the framework of the body"; derived from a Greek word that means "dried up"; odd use: "skeleton in your closet" meaning something hidden from others; 3 syllables; hidden words: *ton, to, let*

∗ **digestion**: word used often in science; means "the process by which food is broken down by the body"; related words: *digest, digestive system*; *-tion* suffix changes verb *digest* into a noun; 3 syllables; hidden words: *digest, dig*

∗ **stomach**: word used often in science; means "the saclike organ in the digestive system where the food is stored until fully digested"; odd uses of the term *stomach*: "butterflies in the stomach" describes being nervous, and "can't stomach that" describes inability to tolerate or like something; /k/ sound made by *ch*; tricky sound made by *o*; 2 syllables; hidden words: *tom, ma, mach* (deals with speed), *to*

∗ **circulation**: word used often in science; means "the continuous movement of blood through the heart and blood vessels"; circulation is how the body's tissues get nutrients, oxygen, and other important secretions and is one way in which waste is carried from the body; related words: *circulate, circulatory system*; word part *circ* means "around"; *-tion* suffix changes verb *circulate* into a noun; 4 syllables

∗ **heart**: word used often in science; names the essential, pump-like organ of the circulatory system that keeps the blood flowing; often referred to as the center of emotion, as in "brokenhearted," or "with all your heart"; related to *cardio* and *cardiac*; rhymes with *-art* words such as *start, chart, smart*; tricky *ea* vowels that are *r*-controlled; hidden words: *hear, ear, art, he*

Day 2: Word Whittle

Distribute the plastic bags containing this week's words or ask students to retrieve them. Have students place the words across the top of their workspace. After you read the first clue, they pull down all the words that fit it. For each subsequent clue in the set, students continue to whittle the words by returning those that don't fit to the top of their workspace. No new words can be added to the group after the first clue. Only one word will remain after the final clue in a set. Students return the word card to the top of their workspace before the next set of clues begins.

First Set:

1. a word that has 3 syllables (*already, skeleton, digestion*)
2. a word that has at least 2 tall letters (*already, skeleton, digestion*)
3. a word that relates to the body (*skeleton, digestion*)
4. a word that names a framework for the body (*skeleton*)

Second Set:

1. a word that starts with a letter that comes before *m* in the alphabet (*already, let's, digestion, circulation, heart*)
2. a word that has a *t* (*let's, digestion, circulation, heart*)
3. a word that has an *e* (*let's, digestion, heart*)
4. a word that is a contraction (*let's*)

Third Set:

1. a word that relates to the body (*skeleton, digestion, stomach, circulation, heart*)
2. a word that names an organ of the body (*stomach, heart*)
3. a word that has both an *h* and a *t* (*stomach, heart*)
4. a word for a part of the circulatory system (*heart*)

Fourth Set:

1. a word that has at least 3 vowels (*already, skeleton, digestion, circulation*)
2. a word that has 2 of the same vowel (*already, skeleton, digestion, circulation*)

3. a word that has 3 syllables (*already, skeleton, digestion*)
4. a word that fits in this sentence: "When we arrived, they had _____ eaten supper." (*already*)

Stump the Class

Give pairs or small groups time to work together to find relationships among this week's words. Once they have found a category into which several of the words fit, they should write the words in a circle on the Word Clusters sheet (see page 127) and the category underneath. Allow time for each pair or group to share one set of their words and ask the rest of the class to guess the category. Even though the other students may suggest a legitimate category, only the presenters' category is the correct answer. The goal is to stump the rest of the class with a unique category. (You might discover categories that you can add to the Day 5: Word Smart activity.)

Day 3: Word Builder

Have students separate the letters at the bottom of this week's word template. Ask them to spell words as you call them out. Have students construct words based on patterns in the words and call out words in increasingly difficult order as shown below. The final word should answer this clue: We don't want it to be seen! (*skeletons*)

toss	lot	leek	note	stole
loss	slot	sleek	notes	stolen
lost	slots	ton	keen	skeletons
lose	not	tone	knee	
loses	knot	stone	knees	
	knots	stones		

As students spell each word, write it on the board. Ask them to cross-check their spelling with yours and correct any errors. On the board or in a pocket chart, sort the words according to the following spelling patterns:

-oss	-ot	-eek	-one
toss	lot	leek	tone
loss	slot	sleek	stone
	not		
	knot		

After all the words have been spelled and sorted, have students read over the list, emphasizing the spelling pattern from the first vowel to the end of each word. In the case of multisyllabic words, the rimes are a bit different, so stress the rhymes of these words.

Tell students that these patterns can help them spell many other words. The Day 4 activity will start with these patterns.

Take an opportunity to talk about some of the following elements: plurals with -s endings; *kn-* where *k* is silent; and the blends *sl-* and *st-*.

Day 4: Rhymer

Return to some of the patterns from the Day 3 lesson. With students, brainstorm a list of words using these rime patterns. This can be done in several different ways:

- The whole group brainstorms with you and makes a list.
- Assign the same or different patterns to partners or small groups. Have them create a list of words to share with the class.
- Make the small-group assignment competitive. Choose a pattern and let each group take turns adding a word to the list until only one group is able to add a word. You might want to let groups use a dictionary to verify their words.

Day 5: Word Smart

Distribute the Lesson 35 words and ask students to arrange them across the top of their desk with plenty of workspace below. Have students respond to your questions by picking up the correct word card(s) and holding it so you can see their answer. If there are more than two correct answers, tell students to show only two—one in each hand. Ask students, "Can you find the . . ."

- word that is a contraction?
- word that rhymes with *smart*? *flight*?
- word that relates to breaking down food in the body?
- word that relates to blood flow throughout the body?
- word that names an organ of the body?
- word that has a suffix that changes the base word into a noun?
- word that means "let us"? "maybe"?
- word that is often used at Halloween? when talking about love?
- word hiding something you do with a shovel?
- word hiding a body part on your head?
- word hiding what you do with that same body part?
- word hiding something you do with a book? to your pizza?
- word hiding something heavy? a measure of speed?
- word that has 4 syllables? 5 vowels? means "strength"?
- word hiding a pronoun for a boy or man?
- word hiding what painters produce?
- word with a word part that means "around"?

❋ Homework ❋

After Day 5, words go home with students. They review the words and use them to complete the Parent-Child Word Work page (see page 128).

been	publish
off	unknown
cold	unlikely
tell	interpret

b e h i l p r s s u

Systematic Word Study for Grades 2–3 © 2011 by Cheryl M. Sigmon, Scholastic Teaching Resources • Lesson 1

work

adjective

first

county

goes

rural

does

urban

a b b n r s u u

them	us
your	compare
their	contrast
pronoun	dissolve

a e i i i i i l m r s s t

Systematic Word Study for Grades 2–3 © 2011 by Cheryl M. Sigmon, Scholastic Teaching Resources • Lesson 3

its	plural
around	fraction
don't	one-fourth
right	one-third

a c f i n o r s t

would

revise

green

conflict

call

landmark

sleep

symbol

a c e k p r r s s y

Systematic Word Study for Grades 2–3 © 2011 by Cheryl M. Sigmon, Scholastic Teaching Resources • Lesson 5

five	edit
wash	resource
know	energy
before	nonrenewable

c e e f l o r r s u u

where	prefixes
were	prewrite
when	distance
or	inches

a e e e m m n r s t u

Systematic Word Study for Grades 2–3 © 2011 by Cheryl M. Sigmon, Scholastic Teaching Resources • Lesson 7

then	draft
could	singular
ask	yard
every	foot

a c e e n p r r s t

write	plot
always	infer
made	investigate
gave	scientist

a e g i i n o r s t t v

 Systematic Word Study for Grades 2–3 © 2011 by Cheryl M. Sigmon, Scholastic Teaching Resources • Lesson 9

very	suffixes
buy	dimensions
those	perimeter
use	circle

d e i i m n n o s s

fast	volunteer
pull	contribution
both	privilege
duty	government

a c c d e m o r y

Systematic Word Study for Grades 2–3 © 2011 by Cheryl M. Sigmon, Scholastic Teaching Resources • Lesson 11

sit

which

read

glossary

evaporation

barometer

atmosphere

cycle

a e e h o m p r s t

why

found

because

economy

distribution

export

import

abbreviation

a a b b e i i n o r s t v

Systematic Word Study for Grades 2–3 © 2011 by Cheryl M. Sigmon, Scholastic Teaching Resources • Lesson 13

best

symmetry

upon

congruent

these

polygon

predict

intersecting

a e i g l n r s t

sing	offspring
wish	parent
many	depend
habitat	heredity

a e e g i n n o r t

 Systematic Word Study for Grades 2–3 © 2011 by Cheryl M. Sigmon, Scholastic Teaching Resources • Lesson 15

if

long

about

product

produce

services

goods

barter

a c g h i p n r s u

got	fiction
six	nonfiction
never	fable
sequential	purpose

e e i m s s r t y

Systematic Word Study for Grades 2–3 © 2011 by Cheryl M. Sigmon, Scholastic Teaching Resources • Lesson 17

seven	organism
eight	consumer
tonight	producer
compost	decomposer

c d e e m p o o r s

myself	opinion
much	angle
keep	parallel
fact	perpendicular

a a c e h i m m t t s

Systematic Word Study for Grades 2–3 © 2011 by Cheryl M. Sigmon, Scholastic Teaching Resources • Lesson 19

try	climate
start	agriculture
highest	scarcity
global	manufacturing

a a c e f m n t r u u

bring

drink

only

declarative

exclamatory

orbit

solar

rotation

a m n o o r s t y

 Systematic Word Study for Grades 2–3 © 2011 by Cheryl M. Sigmon, Scholastic Teaching Resources • Lesson 21

better	imperative
hold	quart
warm	pound
interrogative	ounce

a b e g h m r r s u

full	ancestor
done	ethnic
light	population
culture	artifact

a i l n p p o o u t

Systematic Word Study for Grades 2–3 © 2011 by Cheryl M. Sigmon, Scholastic Teaching Resources • Lesson 23

pick	stanza
cut	endangered
hurt	predator
poetry	prey

a a g i l l o r s t

kind	citation
enough	keyboard
Internet	mouse
reliable	source

a b d e k o r s y

Systematic Word Study for Grades 2–3 © 2011 by Cheryl M. Sigmon, Scholastic Teaching Resources • Lesson 25

carry	area
small	perimeter
table	capacity
possessive	elapsed

a e g g i i n p s u

show

whether

weather

threaten

thrive

thermometer

discuss

beautiful

a c e h i n r r s u

Systematic Word Study for Grades 2–3 © 2011 by Cheryl M. Sigmon, Scholastic Teaching Resources • Lesson 27

far

hemisphere

strange

geography

cause

landforms

effect

arid

e g g i l o o s s t

draw	details
clean	decimal
round	equivalent
conclusion	estimate

a e g i i i m n s t t

Systematic Word Study for Grades 2–3 © 2011 by Cheryl M. Sigmon, Scholastic Teaching Resources • Lesson 29

grow	sentence
together	summarize
thought	example
between	answer

i l n o o s s t u

young	infection
laugh	parasite
family	prescribe
children	physical

a b c i i i n o s t t

 Systematic Word Study for Grades 2–3 © 2011 by Cheryl M. Sigmon, Scholastic Teaching Resources • Lesson 31

inside	frequency
watch	integer
somewhere	infinite
subset	coordinates

a b e i m n r s u

without

highlands

sometimes

erosion

coast

conservation

mountains

prairie

a e e g h i n r t w

 Systematic Word Study for Grades 2–3 © 2011 by Cheryl M. Sigmon, Scholastic Teaching Resources • Lesson 33

strong	eclipse
other	gravity
folktale	fossil
animal	discovery

a d i n o r s s u

might

already

let's

skeleton

digestion

stomach

circulation

heart

e e k l n o s s t

Systematic Word Study for Grades 2–3 © 2011 by Cheryl M. Sigmon, Scholastic Teaching Resources • Lesson 35

Word Clusters

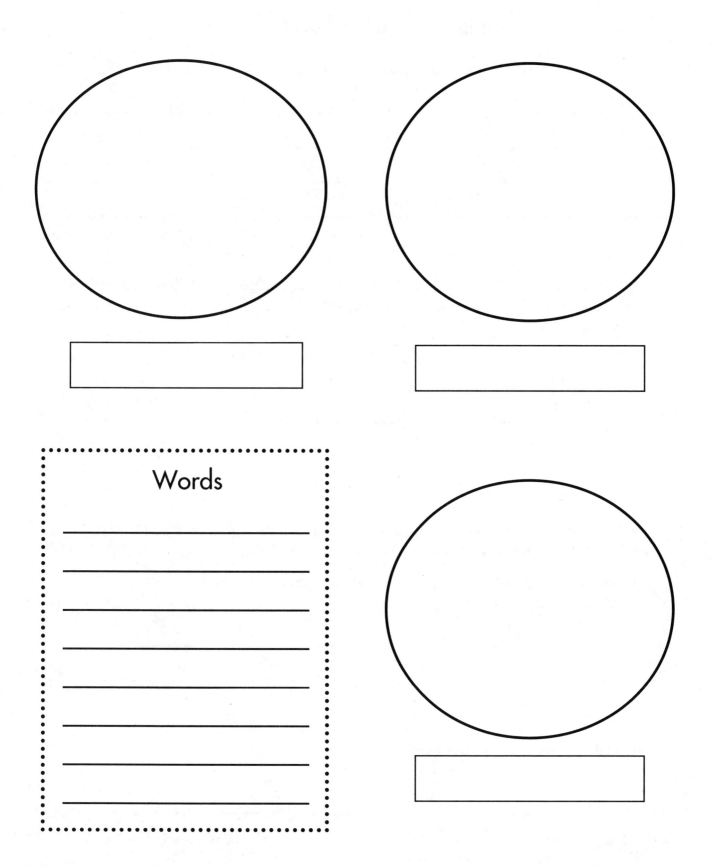

Words

Student Name _____ Date _____

Parent-Child Word Work

I made these words with the letters from this week's mystery word:

_____   _____

_____   _____

_____   _____

_____   _____

Parent: Please review your child's work. Place a ✓ or an ✗ in each box.

☐ My child was able to tell me some features of each word. (Example: sounds, how many tall letters it has or letters that go below the line, how many syllables/claps it has, which little words are hiding inside it, and so on)

☐ My child was able to use each of the 8 words in a sentence.

☐ My child was able to read each of the 8 words.

☐ My child was able to spell these high-frequency words correctly*:

_____   _____

_____   _____

(*Note*: Please do not worry about the correct spelling of words with more than two syllables. At this grade level, knowing the meanings of these words is far more important.)

☐ My child was able to make these new words with these spelling patterns*:
(Example: *-est: best, vest, nest, test*)

_____ : _____

_____ : _____

_____ : _____

☐ **My child got word power this week!**

Parent signature _____ Date _____

* *To the Teacher*: Write the high-frequency words and spelling patterns on the sheet before the student takes it home.